Lee Kelly

Lee Kelly

One through Nine

Randal Davis & Kassandra Kelly

Lee Kelly: One through Nine was published by Leland Iron Works Press, Oregon City, Oregon, in May. 2015.

Designed by Randal Davis.
All artworks copyright Lee Kelly.

"...and how things are put together..." copyright Randal Davis, 2015.
"Introduction to One through Nine" copyright Kassandra Kelly, 2015.

Cover Image: *Seven*, 2014. Oil on canvas, 24 x 24 inches. Collection of the artist.

Printed by CreateSpace

For more information about Lee Kelly go to www.leekellysculpture.net

Contents

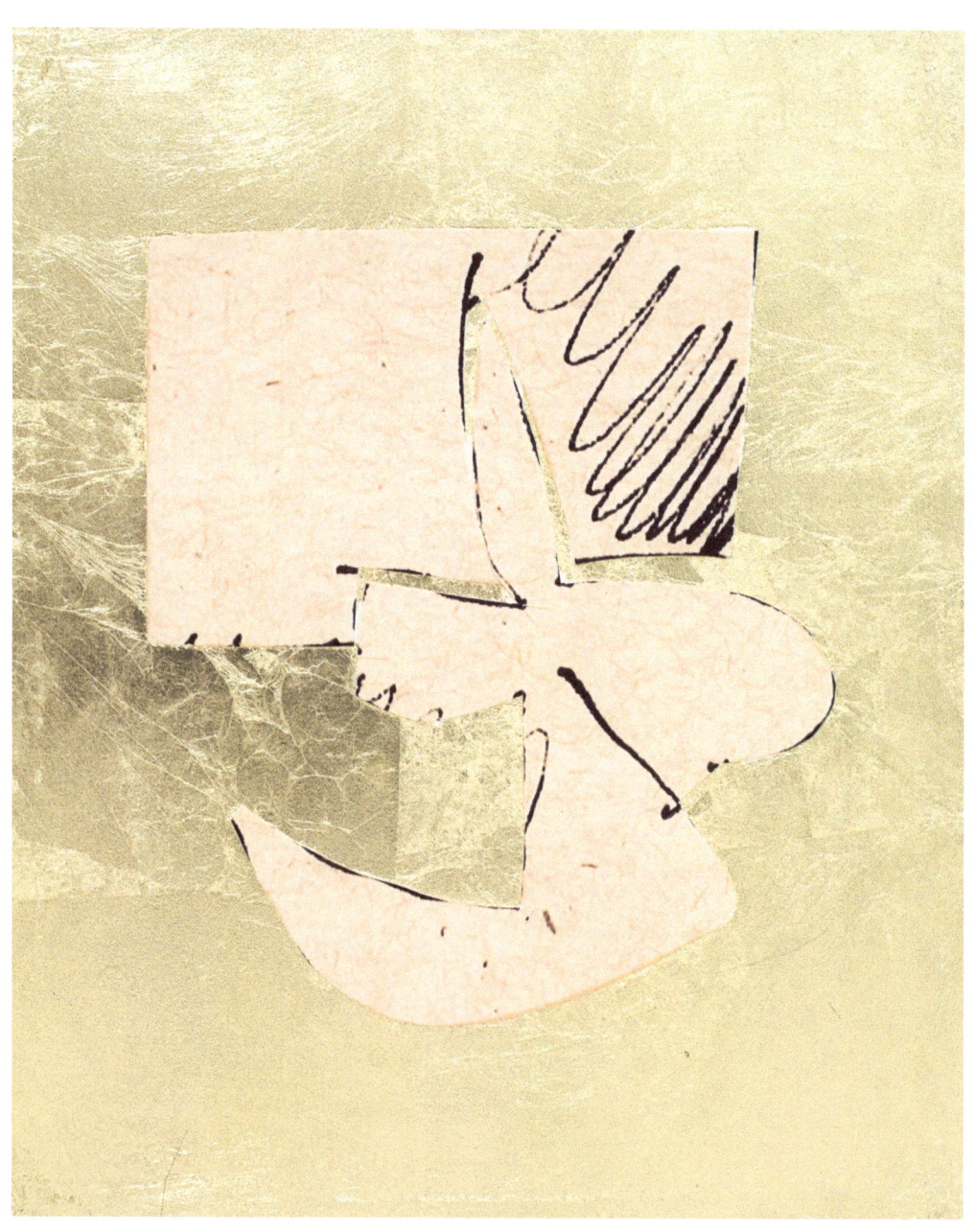

Study for a Painting I 2013
Collage on gesso board with gold leaf, 11 x 9.5 inches
Collection of the artist

When I lived and studied in Ohio, I had a very vague sense of what art was....

Genuine oil painting was some highly cultivated act that came like the silver spoon, born from years of slow method, applied drawing, watercoloring, designing, art structure, requiring special equipment of an almost secret nature, that could only be found in Paris or possibly New York, and when I got to New York and Paris I found that painting was made with anything at hand, building board, raw canvas, self-primed canvas, with or without brushes, on the easel, on the floor, on the wall, no rules, no secret equipment, no anything, except the conviction of the artist, his challenge to the world and his own identity.

David Smith, "Tradition and Identity"

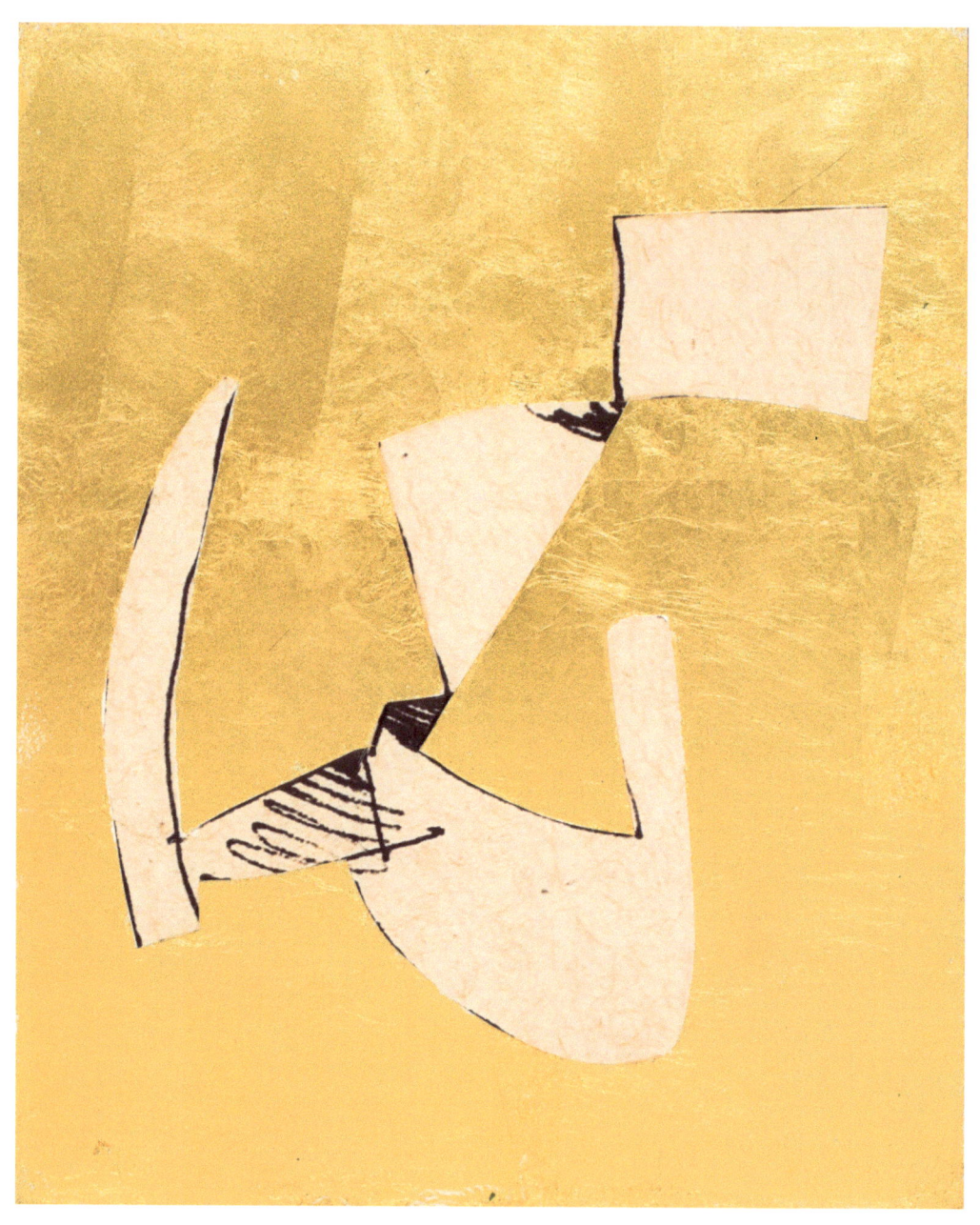

Study for a Painting I 2013
Collage on gesso board with gold leaf, 11 x 9.5 inches
Collection of the artist

Introduction to *One through Nine*   **Kassandra Kelly**

Randal Davis and I often make books for my father's birthday. Lee Kelly's yearly artistic production cannot usually be contained in a single volume, but we like to take a moment each year to say something about what we have seen during the last twelve months.

We assembled the first book in 2011 after Lee's retrospective exhibition at the Portland Art Museum. At that time, Randal wanted to look closely at Lee's sculpture since 1990. The museum's catalog essay on the retrospective focused on Lee's work from the 1960s through the 1980s, which included some of Lee's most innovative and controversial work. But there was little mention of his work after 1990.

1990 is a natural dividing line in Lee's career. His wife, Bonnie Bronson, died in that year. Some sculptures made during this time, such as the *Bonnie Quartet*, have never been examined critically. Or even left his studio property. Other dividing lines exist in his work that I can recognize because, as his daughter, I've known him so long. When he stopped painting on canvas – 1963 – after moving to his new studio in Oregon City. When my brother died – 1978 – which appears in Lee's large Cor-ten sculptures of that era as a soft edged shadow. When he started fabricating intricate Tibetan knots in stainless steel – 1980 – after his first visit to Nepal. And his great wall sculptures of the 1990s and 2000s created after visits to Sulawesi, New Zealand, Cambodia and other places.

The biggest wind change, and the one people will point to in years to come, is Lee's return to painting on canvas. It started after his original paintings from 1958 to 1963 came to light again. They had been stored in open racks in the top floor of his studio for decades. After the grime was removed, the paintings were dazzling. And suddenly there was an audience for work that had been forgotten for over fifty years.

I doubt if Lee rested easily with this development. Although the paintings were his, he must have felt almost as though he was in competition with his younger self. Maybe there was a spark in his mind that said, "Fuck it. I can paint better than that." And *One through Nine* came from this spark.

Randal will tell you in the next essay, however, that these new paintings did not rise out of Lee's Abstract Expressionist past. They are not a return to the older work. In fact they emerged from his sculptural work of the last ten to 15 years. Though it is tempting to make *One through Nine* another dividing line in Lee's career, it is impossible to say exactly when it started. Settled times are never as interesting or well differentiated as tragic times. To get the story, sometimes it is necessary to step back and view the whole thing. And even then, you may find yourself in the middle of it, no end in sight. So I invite you to look at and enjoy the images in this book. It's not what you think you know about Lee.

It's better.

One through Nine

One 2014
Oil on canvas, 68 x 60 inches
Collection of the artist

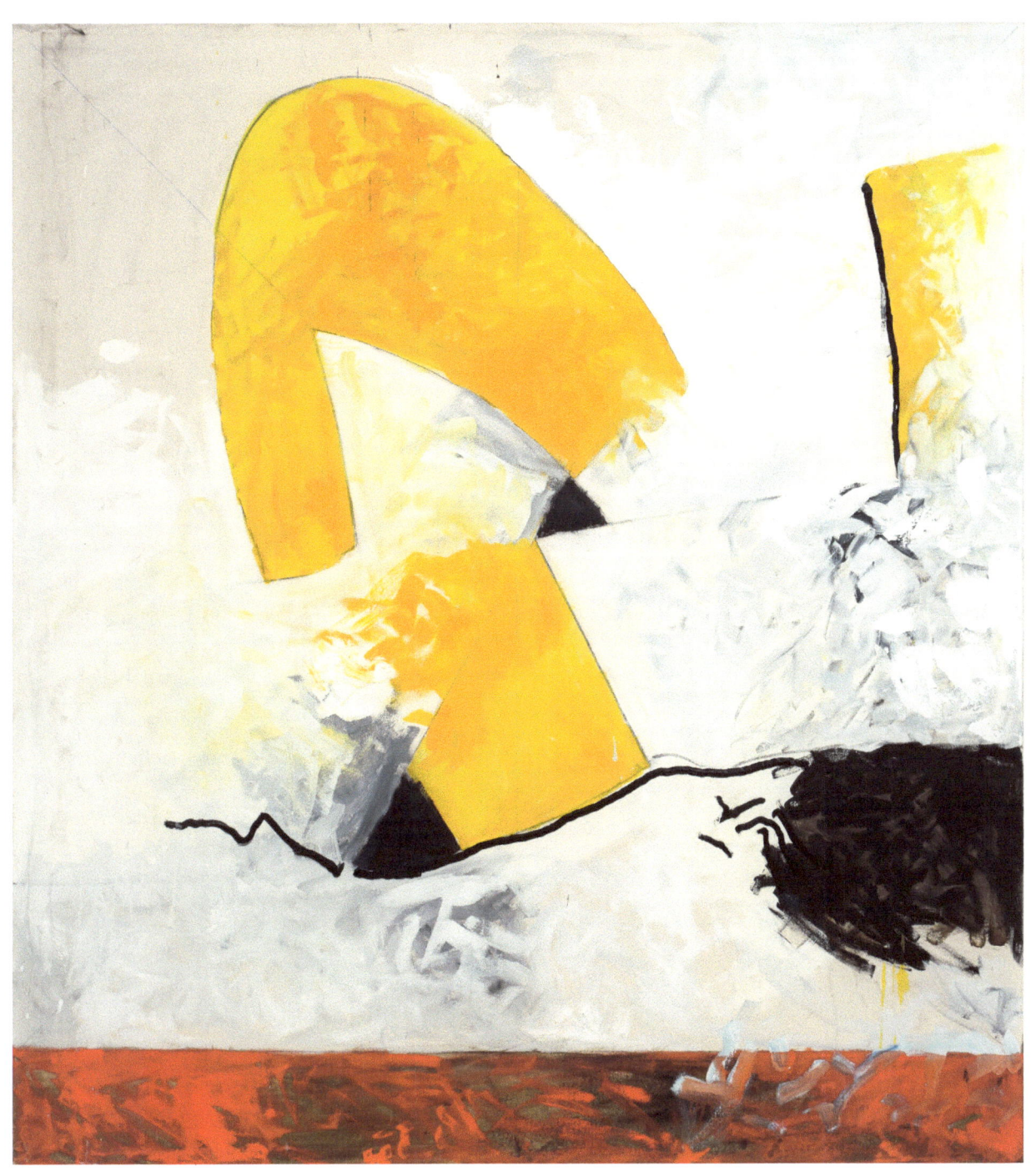

Two 2014
Oil on canvas, 68 x 60 inches
Collection of the artist

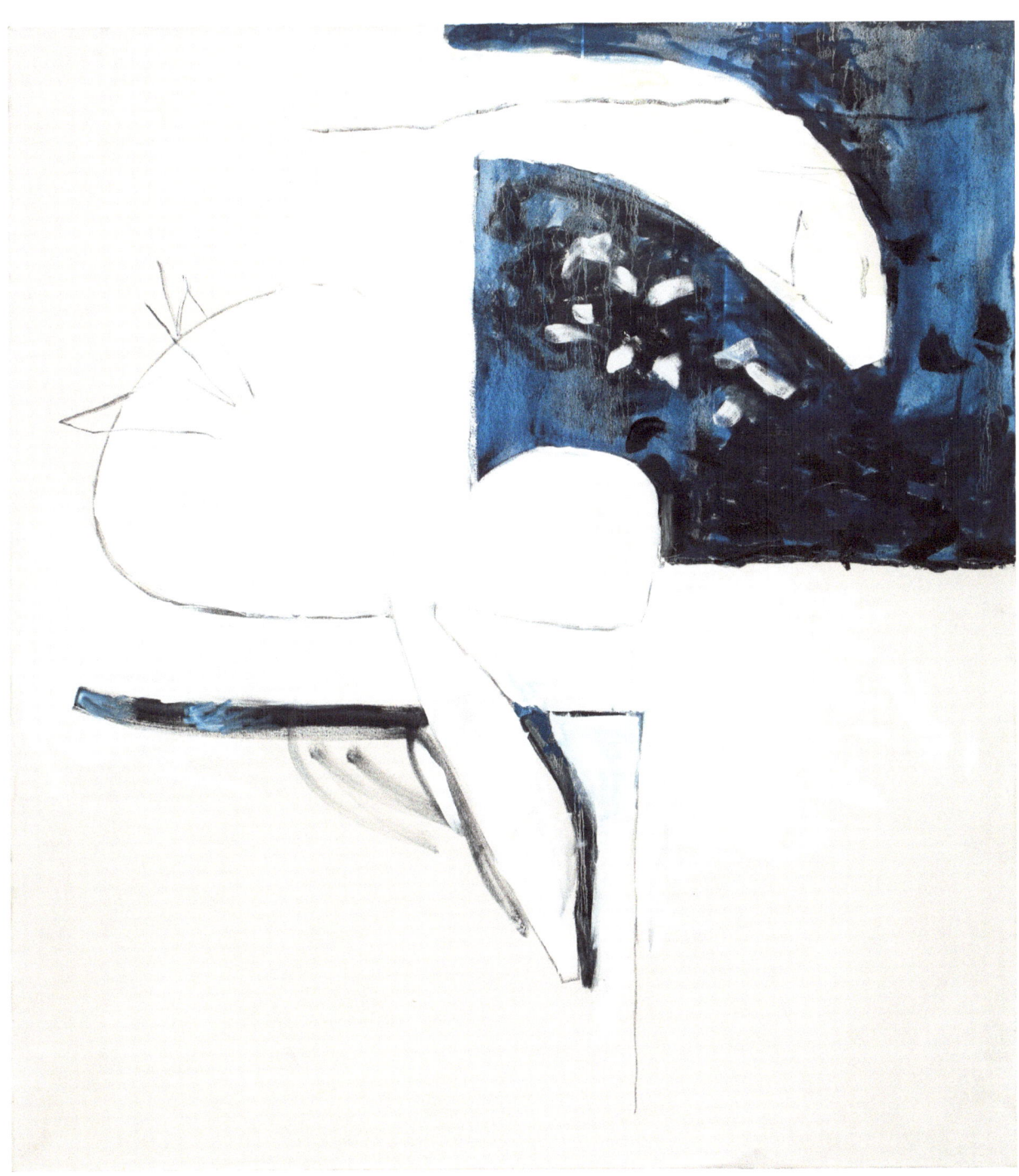

Three 2014
Oil on canvas, 68 x 60 inches
Collection of Mark & Ann Edlen

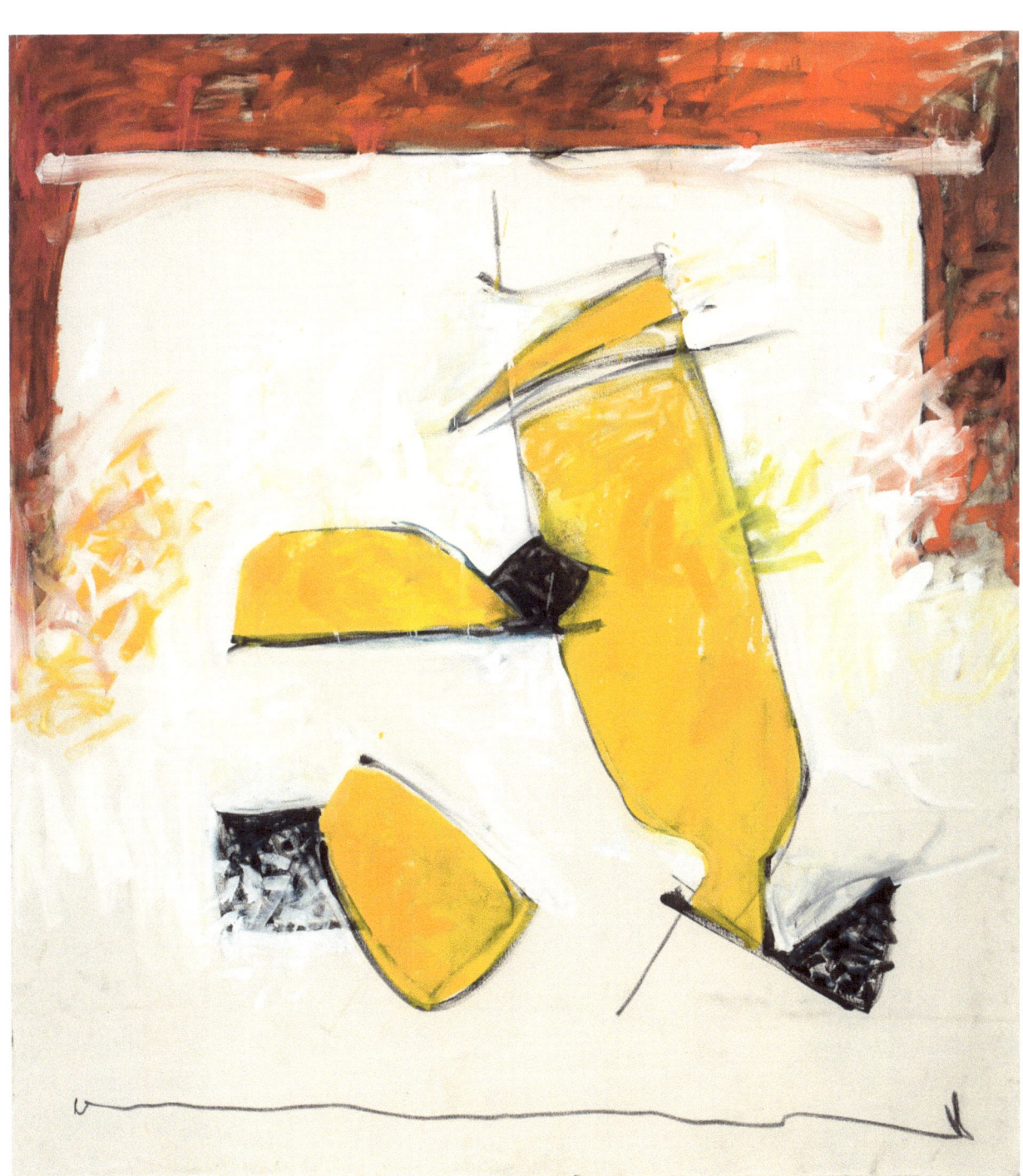

Four 2014
Oil on canvas, 24 x 24 inches
Collection of the artist

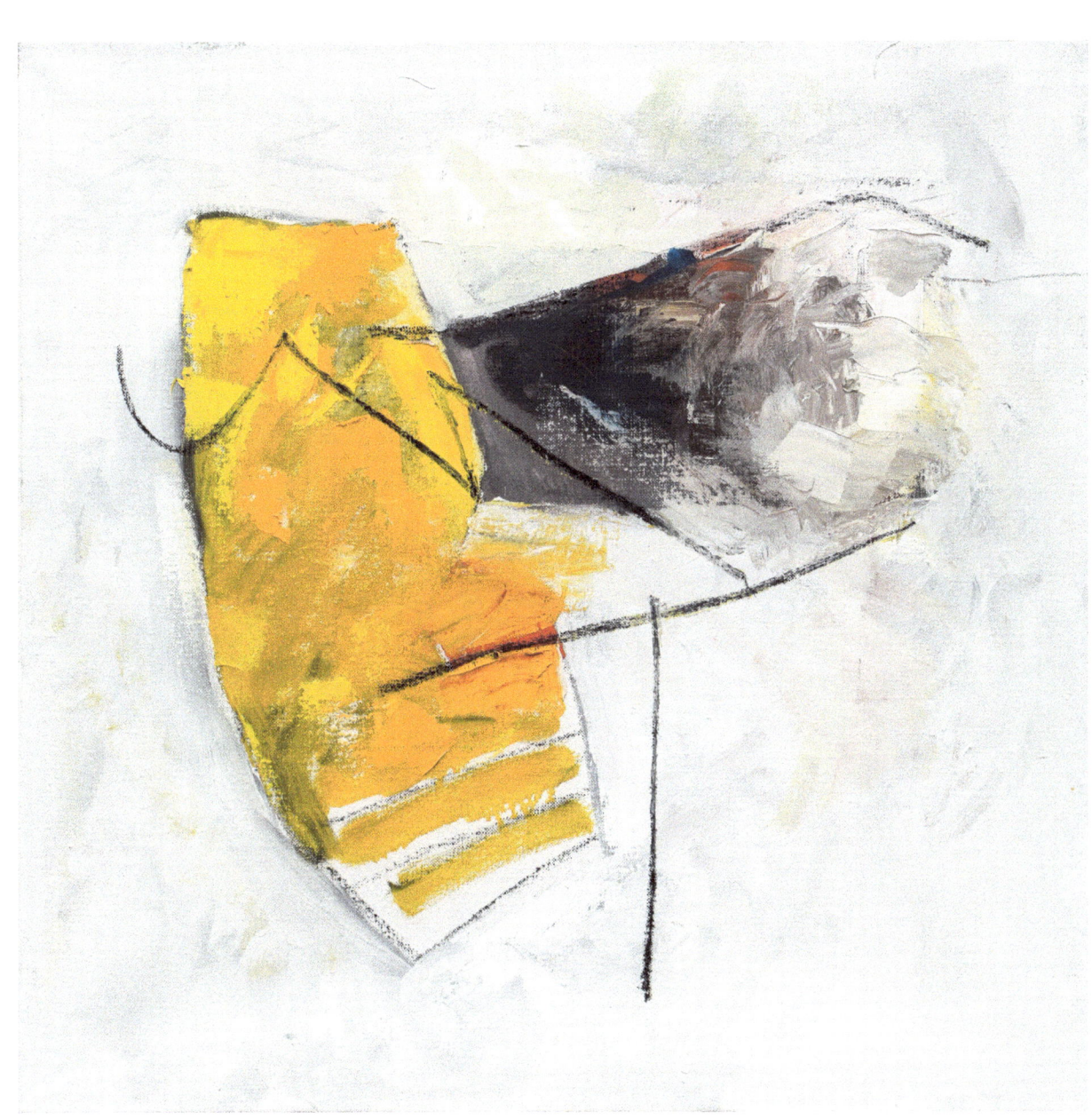

Five 2014
Oil on canvas, 24 x 24 inches
Collection of the artist

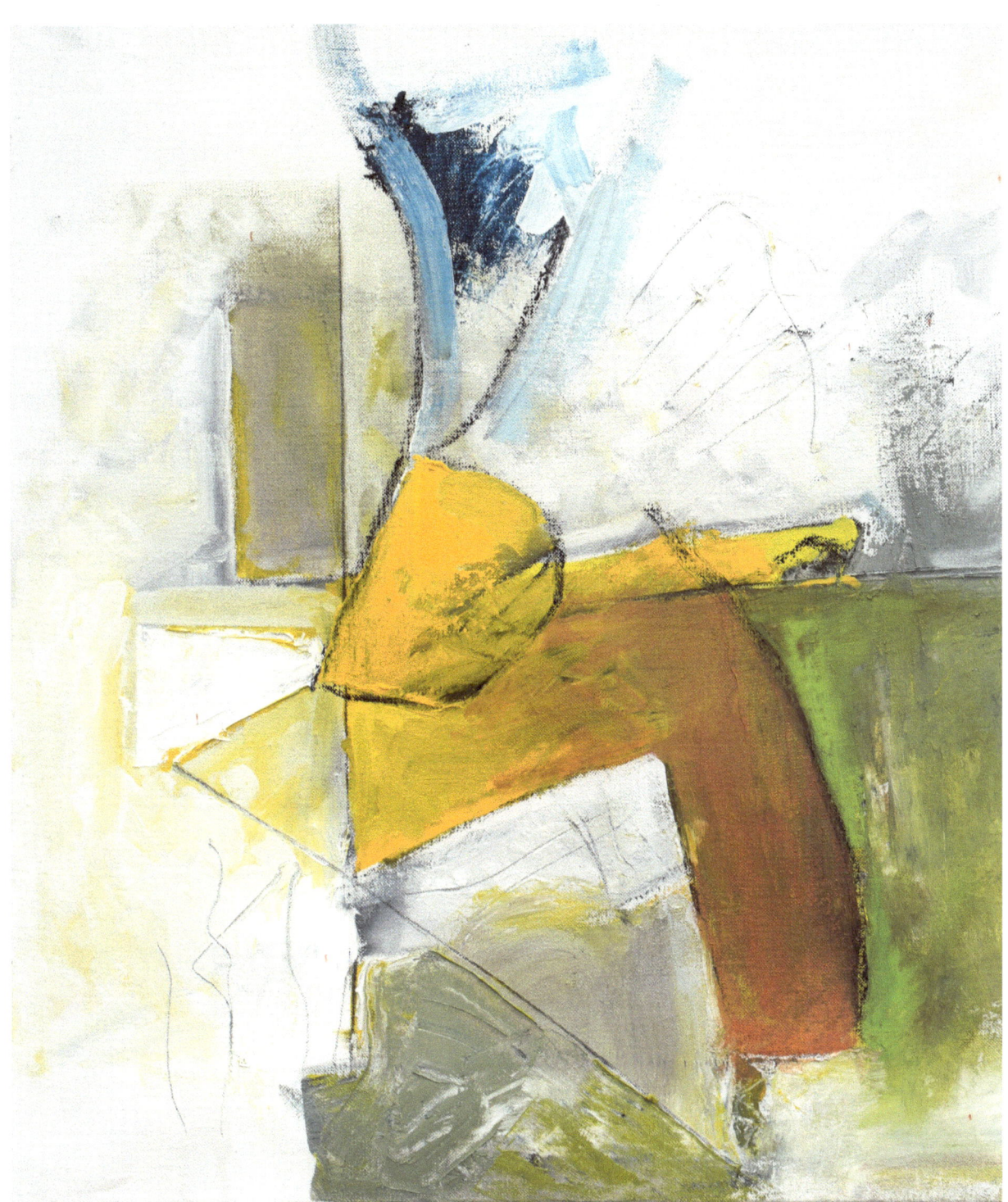

Six 2014
Oil on canvas, 24 x 24 inches
Collection of the artist

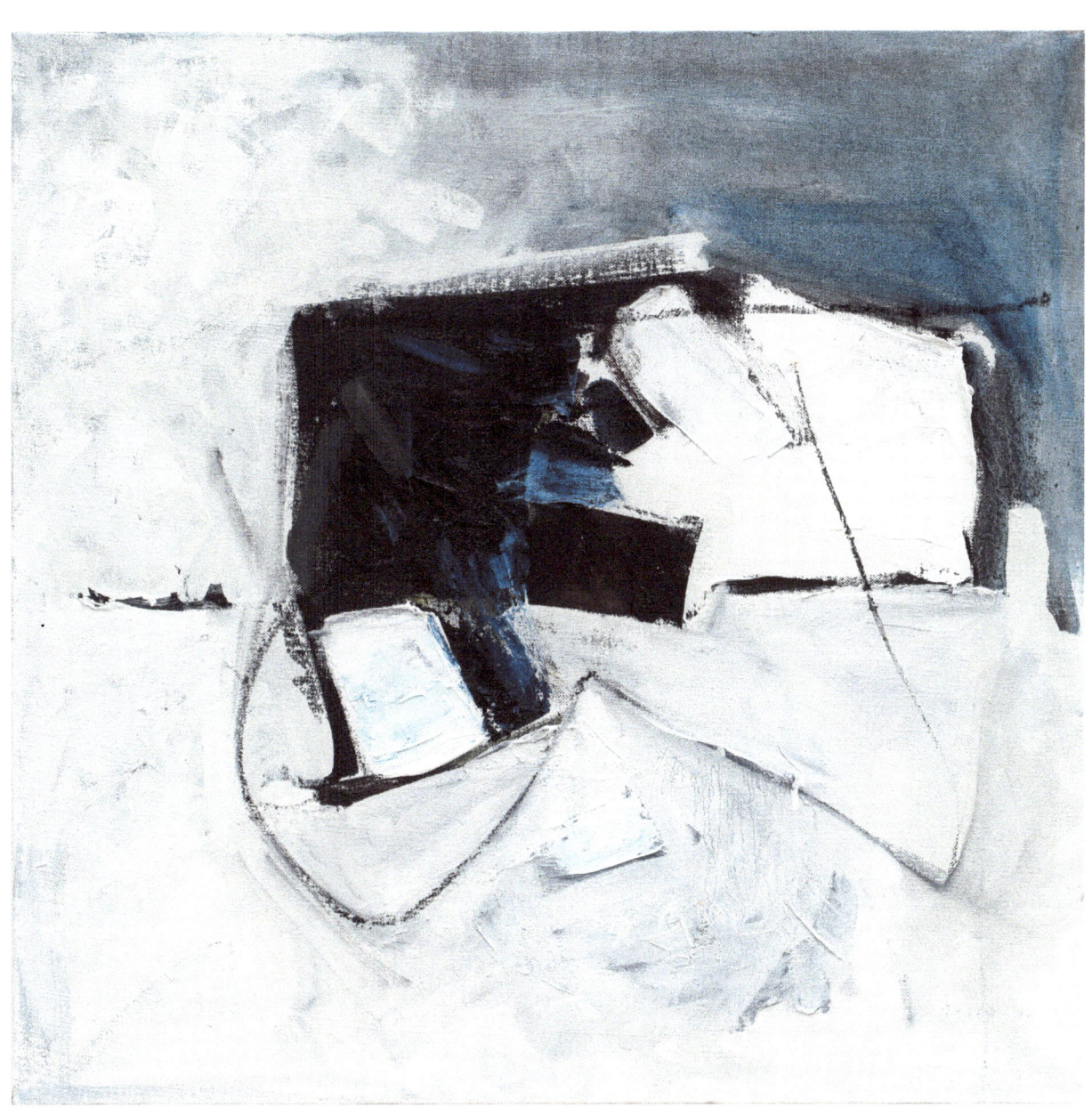

Seven 2014
Oil on canvas, 24 x 24 inches
Collection of the artist

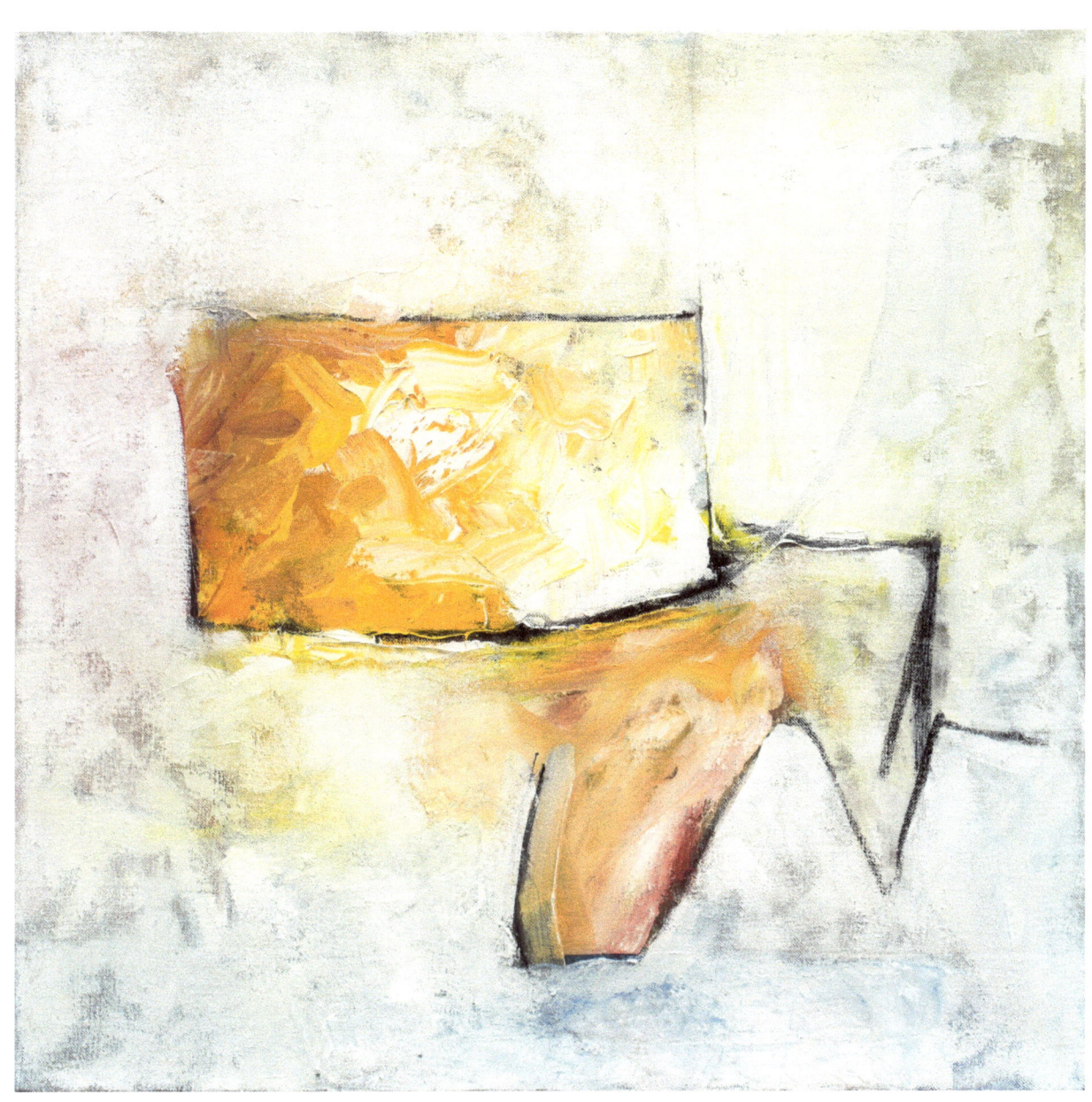

Eight 2014
Oil on canvas, 24 x 24
Collection of the artist

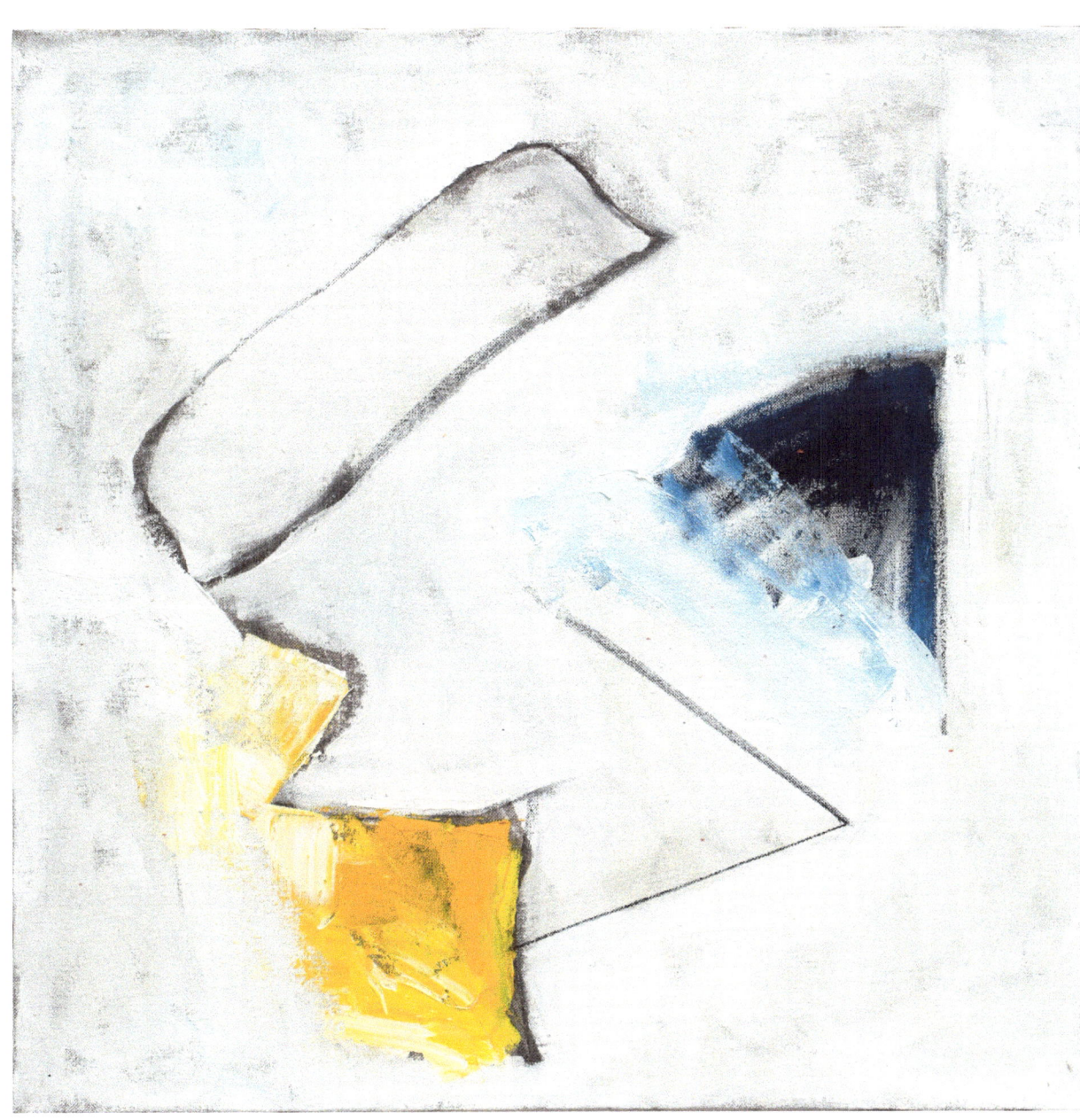

Nine 2013
Oil on canvas, 24 x 24 inches
Collection of the artist

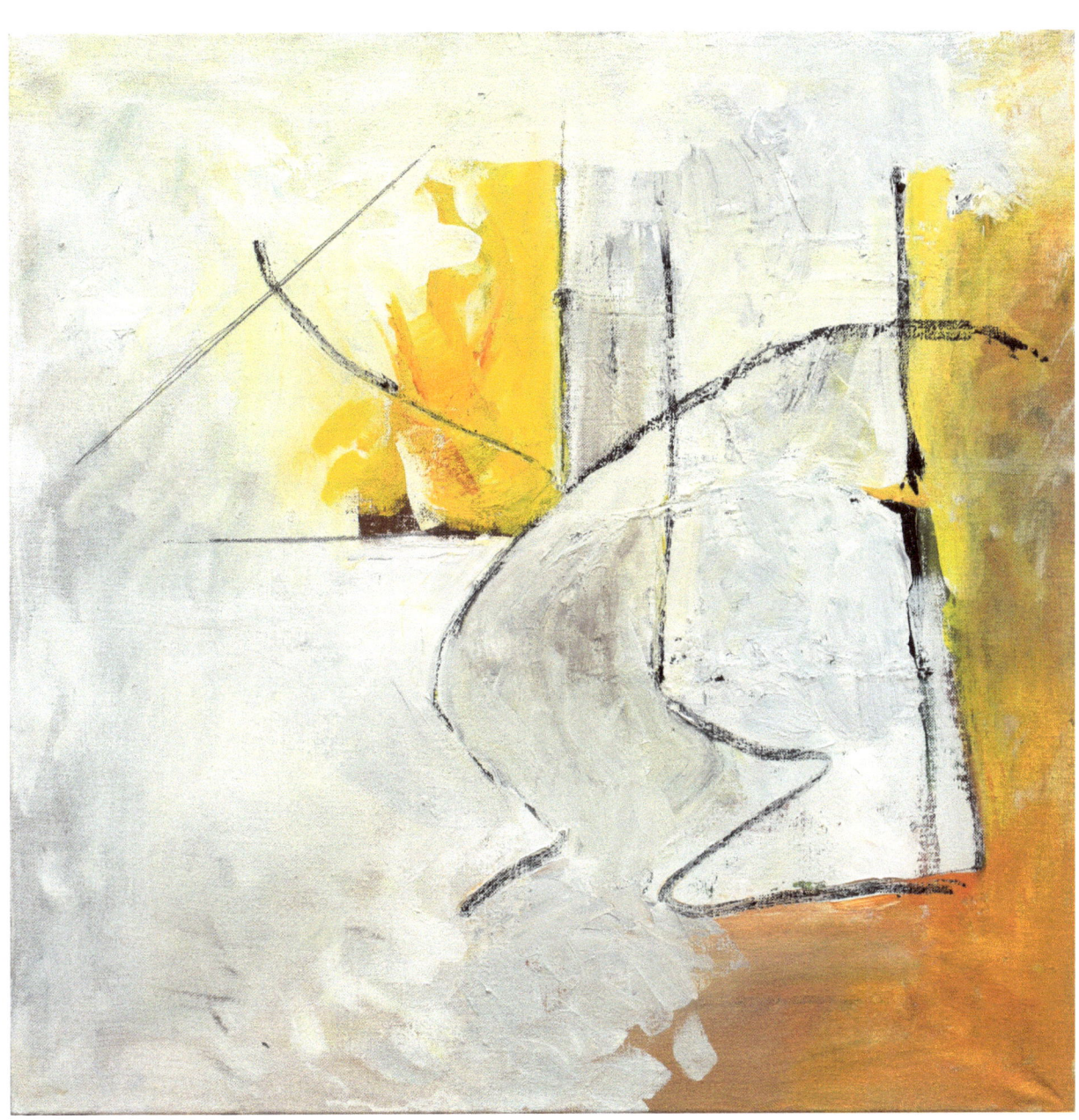

"...and how things are put together..."   **Randal Davis**

> A picture is not thought out and settled beforehand. While it is being done, it changes as one's
> thoughts change. And when it is finished it still goes on changing, according to the state of mind
> of whoever is looking at it. A picture lives a life like a living creature, undergoing the changes
> imposed on us by our own life from day to day.
>
> Pablo Picasso

For over five decades, Lee Kelly has been widely recognized as one of the Pacific Northwest's pre-eminent artists, an acclaim largely founded on extensive bodies of work in both stainless steel and Cor-ten steel, often at monumental scale. His 2008 exhibition with Elizabeth Leach Gallery, his long-time representative, was a sort of golden jubilee – his first major solo exhibition had been at Marylhurst College in 1958. *Doubtful Sound* brought back a number of paintings from that period, as well as the eponymous series of then-recent wall sculptures. For those at least relatively recent to Lee Kelly's work, *Doubtful Sound* illuminated the not altogether effortless passage from painting to sculpture.

Born in 1932, Kelly is roughly one generation younger than the first generation of Abstract Expressionist painters. Hardly surprising, then, considering the hegemony of what was the International Style of painting, that he began his career within that idiom. D.K. Row provided an overview of the works from this early career:

> Kelly is primarily known as a sculptor trained in architecture. But he began his career as a painter, and
> a casual look at this exhibit's painted abstract blooms of red, orange, blue, white and other colors show
> that some 40 years ago, Kelly was struggling with the one movement every artist confronted at that time:
> abstract expressionism... Kelly was channeling jazz, on one level, while experimenting with form and color,
> struggling to refine a new language of visual expression.

His most recent exhibition with Leach, *Pavilion* (2014), reprised an admixture of painting and sculpture, but with a striking difference; in this case, all of the works had been executed within the previous year, including a remarkable series of nine paintings. The sculptures in *Pavilion* were easily recognized within Kelly's recent formal vocabulary, combining architectural referents with stylized figuration.

But the paintings were something else again, constituting a significant body of truly new work. In one sense, of course, how could that not be the case? He had effectively abandoned painting by the early 1960s, some fifty years earlier. Put differently, that the series of paintings *One through Nine* was something new is finally less surprising than, say, taking up the brush precisely where you left off fifty years ago.

This is not to suggest that two-dimensional work has not been an important part of his practice. Quite the contrary, and I advance a five-point topology: technical drawings, studies, what I call "imaginings," low-relief pictorial sculptures and, finally, paintings. Although my nominal subject here is the latter, emphasizing the connections between these works, rather than the differences, is necessary. That is to say, having proposed a series of distinctions, I am less interested in how the system differentiates Kelly's production than what we might call its "porosity," a permeability showing how one aspect of the work leads to another.

Consider, for example, the superficially transparent example of formal structural drawings. Even a passing acquaintance with Kelly's work since the mid-70's makes evident that the large works could not have been fabricated without preparation of architectural resolution. But this was not always the case. When Kelly began to move his studio practice from painting to sculpture, the work process was very different.

On the occasion of his 1994 retrospective at Marylhurst College, Paul Sutinen addressed this: "Kelly's sculpture was also painted, not after the fact of making the form, but during the process. He would weld, paint, weld some more. 'Paint would bubble up around the edges' [Kelly recalled] as he welded." Put differently, Kelly's transition from painting to sculpture at least initially retained much of the brash improvisation of his gestural abstractions.

Many artists make preliminary studies for work, whether 2-or 3-dimensional, and Kelly is no exception, as amply evidenced by the *Kyoto* series. Likenesses may be obvious, but that is exactly not the point. The *Kyoto Eight* (2007) collages qualify as "studies" conventionally, but to focus on the formal identity neglects their autonomy. The *Kyoto* wall sculptures (also 2007) are dense and cannot appear as other than dramatic gestures within the white box. The mixed media *Kyoto Eight* propose quite a different visual experience. The primary form is rendered lightly, indeed almost impressionistically, against a richly textured ground of metallic leaf that could by no account be construed as a neutral surface.

So, are these studies or autonomous works? Indeed, the titles of the two series of works suggest their independence and, in any case, we cannot always be certain even of precedence. The conventional narrative would, of course, have the "study" in advance of the "major" work, but one need only think of the example of Jasper Johns to see how readily this is confounded. Even if formally identical, the figure ground relation is so radically different that one must question the correspondence of the two sets.

This leads to Kelly's two-dimensional oeuvre as it relates to the formal vocabulary of a sculpture series without actually matching. Something like that obtains in the two sets of studies for paintings reproduced here. There is little doubt that they are "of a piece" with *One through Nine*, yet there are no instances of precise congruence. This apparent independence from the "realized" versions still raises questions. If the six studies have not found their way to the paintings does this mean they are failed attempts? Autonomous thoughts? Or simply preparation for, say, *Ten through Fifteen*?

The *Goddess Glyphs* (2009) are interesting here. Executed as a series, they are, in one sense, a unique series. Manifestly related to one another – note the mirroring in I and II – the gestural vocabulary is still generally consistent with works from *Kyoto* to *One through Nine*, but it would be hard to imagine a greater contrast than what obtains between the luminosity of *One through Nine* and the ruddy grounds of the *Goddess Glyphs* with their gleaming metallic leaf.

A bit thick for their otherwise modest scale, the *Goddess Glyphs* assert a strong object presence. Assembled in the manner of a collage, resolute flatness renders them an essentially pictorial event. They share this property with the otherwise almost wholly dissimilar *Bone's Boxes* [2009], what I referred to earlier as a "low relief pictorial" space. Unwieldy terminology, perhaps, but the meaning becomes clear when comparing, say, *Bone's Boxes* to *Doubtful Sound* [2008]. The structural similarities are evident, but it is again a question of figure and ground. The *Doubtful Sound* works, in either their painted or gilded versions, exercise a strong object presence. *Bone's Boxes*, using what is essentially the same formal language, moves toward a dematerialization. Figure and ground are treated almost interchangeably, and even though the composition as a whole is contained within a frame, the frame itself (the front edge of the box) is treated as part of the work.

Frank O'Hara famously remarked, in discussing the strategies David Smith used in finishing the surfaces of his works,"[...] it is never sculpture being painting, it is sculpture looking at painting and responding to it in its own fashion." This is classic O'Hara, at once a restatement of a central tenet of formalist modernism a la Clement Greenberg but also intimating the possibility of another kind of after-hours meeting. Lee Kelly himself recalled, in conversation with Paul Sutinen regarding his early polychrome free metal constructions, "I remember other artists getting real upset when I painted sculpture. Paint was supposed to be on canvas."

The importance of O'Hara's insight for the paintings of *One through Nine* consists in the possibility of the reversal of its terms. That is, I would propose to say of *One through Nine* that "they are not paintings being sculpture but paintings looking at sculpture and responding in their own fashion." In this view, the series is understood as a summation of their [wall] sculptural counterparts, but from the vantage of a different medium.

This is premised on two fundamental points. One is already heard in many of the notes above on the two-dimensional work, the way in which formal likenesses are found in radically different relations of figure and ground. The second has not yet played a large role in the discussion, but will occupy much of the rest of these notes, as I think it is central not just to these most recent works, but much of Kelly's work for the last three decades. By this I point to the confounding of abstraction and representation in his work.

This is not to suggest that he is not, at least as nominally understood, an abstract artist. David Smith again provides an example, as his work, with that of Anthony Caro, are the obvious origins of Kelly's formal language. Smith always identified as an abstract artist while resolutely maintaining that his artwork was the most profound expression of his identity. At the same time, many commentators on his work, notably Rosalind Krauss, recognized the frequency of figural references in his sculpture. Krauss, specifically citing the *Tanktotems*, saw:

> Yet, in the very way that the image is brought into existence, one feels confronted not so much by a sur-rogate for figural presence as by an abstract sign for it.... the work locates itself at a strange border halfway between the human figure and the abstract sign.

I want to return to my earlier point, what I called a certain confounding of the notional distinction of abstraction and representation. This, of course, is precisely the territory marked by Krauss's "strange border." If we follow this lead there develops a sense in which this is not just a con-founding, in the way of a confusion or mystification, but a co-founding, a sign operating simultaneously in the two very different registers.

Take, for example, the eccentric circle of the large *Sulphur Butterfly* (2006). One might see the central volume as a "body" with two wings to either side, but this is surely somewhat fanciful and may, finally, not really provide much of interest. But if you imagine that stainless steel could be stretched and folded in topological transformations, you see that it is possible to arrive at something very much like the *Goddess Revisited* (2009) works, which are closer to a certain figural presence than the butterfly. Then, as a next step, it's clear that what *Sulphur Butterfly* and *Goddess Revisited* share, an essentially circular form, also produces the elemental figures that stand on the platforms of *Pavilion I* and *Pavilion II* (2013) by means of vertical elongation. But there are other transformations possible as well – more radical deformations of the *Goddess Revisited* forms results in the asymmetries of *Pumalin* (2012).

Part of what I mean by "simultaneity" is that articulation takes place before it has travelled far through the garden of forking paths, the multiplicity that makes individuation possible. And this makes the imagery of *One through Nine* so striking. But perhaps it is yet too soon to call them "images;" let's pull back a bit and call them "geometries." They are, in effect, contextualizing the wall sculptures of recent years, the "primary structures" of Kelly's formal vocabulary.

I use the term advisedly and not without irony as it was the title of one of the landmark exhibitions of minimalism, curated by Kynaston McShine for the Jewish Museum in 1966. Kelly's relation to minimal and postminimal practice is complex, well beyond my scope here. It can, though, be said that, even at his most austere, Kelly has always stood plainly apart from the reductionism of Andre, Flavin and Judd. But, again, this is the subject for another occasion.

If we stay for a moment in 1966, the question becomes clear. It was indeed a watershed year, as Lucy Lippard followed *Primary Structures* with her own group exhibition, *Eccentric Abstraction*; including, among others, Louise Bourgeois, Eva Hesse, Bruce Nauman and Keith Sonnier, Eccentric Abstraction became one of the foundations of postminimalism. In her notes on the exhibition for New York's Fischbach Gallery Lippard wryly observed that "the rigors of structural art would seem to preclude entirely any aberration toward the exotic."

Since Kelly abandoned the massed rectilinear forms characterizing the 1970s and early 1980s, working instead with ever-more prominent curvilinear forms, there is a very real sense in which all of the last three decades is, in Lippard's terms, an "aberration toward the exotic." That is principally because the work now far more directly reflects his travels and passionate involvement with a broad range of cultural referents, notably Meso-American and South Asian. This is not pastiche but rather a synthetic – in the same sense the term is used in cubism-or, better still, a syncretic postmodernism.

One of the signature pieces of this aspect of Kelly's work is the monumental *Akbar's Elephant* (2000). The piece is far more explicit than the implied form of *Sulphur Butterfly* and, perhaps because of this, despite its daunting scale and imposing surface, *Akbar's Elephant* is somewhat light-hearted, almost whimsical. But *Akbar* is, in Krauss's terms, a "strange elephant." Actually, what *Akbar's Elephant* proposes is neither an abstraction nor idealization nor even a cartoon but something like what architect Peter Eisenman calls a "diagram."

> Though it is an ideogram, it is not necessarily an abstraction. It is a representation of something in that it is
> not the thing itself. In this sense it cannot help but be embodied.

Thus does Eisenman conclude, somewhat mysteriously, traversing the strange border, that "a diagram is neither a structure nor an abstraction of structure."

A particularly clear instance of this is found, again, in *Pavilion I* and *Pavilion II*. A formal device that has played an occasional role in Kelly's work at least since *Torana Gateway* (1982), it appears in the two *Pavilions* as two adjacent or adjoining vertical "columns" topped by contrary facing fragments of arches, in the case of both the earlier and later works, approximately 45 degrees of arc. In *Torano Gateway*, their serial progression through Seattle's Union Square cannot but suggest a colonnade. In isolation, though, as in *Pavilion*, they are more ambiguous, the partial arc guaranteeing undecidability. Colonnade? A pair of isolated arches? Or a highly stylized tree?

In this contest, *One through Nine* might appear strikingly reductive and simply refers to the Abstract Expressionism that Kelly abandoned long ago. But that leaves too much unsaid. It is true that the works do not, in general, display the overt play with abstraction and representation that we have seen elsewhere in his recent work, though the seated figure of *Five* is a notable exception. Interestingly, the closest formal analog to *One through Nine* is the 40-foot wall sculptural commission *Moontrap* (2011) – and I will turn to this by way of conclusion.

But we must first note the radical change in Kelly's paint handling in these new works. On the late 1950s and early 1960s, Bruce Guenther saw a "[...] response to paint... muscular and immediate." The result, he noted, was a "roiling surface" animated by "improvisational, hooking brushstrokes and scumbling veils of pigment build[ing] a dense, often opaque, surface of condensed forms."

What is important about this assessment is both what it is and what it isn't. Guenther captures the early paintings well, but it is impossible to imagine this applying to *One through Nine*. To be sure, the works remain at least within "post-painterly abstraction," but the stylistic referents have changed emphatically.

And, then, there is the light.

There are moments of great intensity in the early paintings, much in the Hofmann manner, but almost nothing like the encompassing luminosity suffusing *One through Nine*. The somewhat overheated milieu Guenther evokes is strikingly absent from these recent paintings. What you see most is canvas. Kelly prepared the grounds of the paintings only minimally, and the tooth of the fabric remains very present. This is essential as it sets a stage for overtly painterly events – the red "horizon" in *One* or the "frame" in *Three*. Look also to the richly colored quadrants of *Two* and *Five*, and precisely when you might expect them to come forward, they remain back. But that is also a part of another aspect of reference new to these works – the black and white masses of *Six* cannot but evoke Franz Kline, and his insistence, "I paint the white as well as the black, and the white is just as important."

There is line, of course, but it is very different here than what Guenther saw. In *One through Nine*, it is frequently difficult, as so often with Cy Twombly, to draw clear distinction between marks on the surface and marks of the surface. *Nine* is particular rich, as is the upper right center of *Five*. And it is there that I return to the relation of *Moontrap* to *One through Nine*. Apart from its scale, *Moontrap* would seem very different from many of the other wall sculptures here – it is far more hard-edged and might seem, at least superficially far more explicitly and reductively rectilinear.

But that's not really true, and think again of Kline. *Moontrap* is an extended essay in the relation of figure and ground, positive and negative space. Kelly contemplated this commission for some time, and it could hardly have escaped him that the highly burnished staiuless steel would be set against raw concrete. In high sun, the contrast is dramatic. In more typical conditions of overcast and rain, we again consider the relation of figure and ground. I want to return to Eisenman, and how he developed his idea of the diagram to what he called "superposition." This is, he wrote, "a coextensive, horizontal layering where there is no stable ground or origin, where ground and figure fluctuate between one another."

Yes, *Moontrap* is flanked by two clear verticals, but the complexity of internal continuities and discontinuities between the elements is sufficient to at least imply that the piece could as well have been 400 as 40 feet long. It is about how these elements fit together, what connects, what is left out. And the more you look at the piece the more you realize that some of the best parts were left out. This is what I meant with the suggestion that the paintings of *One through Nine* are elemental to his recent work. It's not about revisiting familiar ground, the old tropes and gestures. It's asking the only question that matters, the one that remains. How do you put things together?

Works cited

Barr, Alfred Hamilton. *Picasso: Forty Years of His Art*. New York: Museum of Modem Art in collaboration with Art Institute of Chicago, 1939.

Eisenman, Peter. "'Diagram: An Original Scene of Writing" in Peter Eisenman, *Diagram Diaries*. New York: Universe Publishing, 1999.

Guenther, Bruce. *Lee Kelly: A Retrospective*. Portland: Portland Art Museum, 2010.

Krauss, Rosalind. *Passages in Modern Sculpture*. Cambridge: MIT Press, 1977.

Lippard, Lucy. "Eccentric Abstraction," *Art International X:9* (November 1966). First published by Fischbach Gallery (New York, October 1966) for the exhibition of the same title.

O'Hara, Frank. "David Smith: The Color of Steel" in Donald Allen (editor), *Standing Still and Walking in New York*. Bolinas: Grey Fox Press, 1974. Originally appeared in Art News (December 1961).

Row, D.K. "Lee Kelly at Elizabeth Leach Gallery," *The Oregonian* (9 August 2008).

Smith, David. "Tradition and Identity," in Garnett McCoy (editor), *David Smith*. New York: Praeger Publishers, 1973. Originally given as a speech in 1959 at Ohio University.

Sutinen, Paul. *Living in Sculpture–The Studio Work of Lee Kelly: Lee Kelly-Thirty-five Years of Painting and Sculpture 1959-1994*. Marylhurst: The Art Gym, Marylhurst College, 1994.

Special thanks to Elizabeth Leach and Gwendolyn Schrader at Elizabeth Leach Gallery for registrarial assistance.

Related Works

Akbar's Elephant 2000
Stainless steel, 184 x 147 x 106 inches
Collection of the artist

Sulphur Butterfly 2006
Stainless steel with gold leaf, 96 x 87 x 24 inches
Collection of the artist

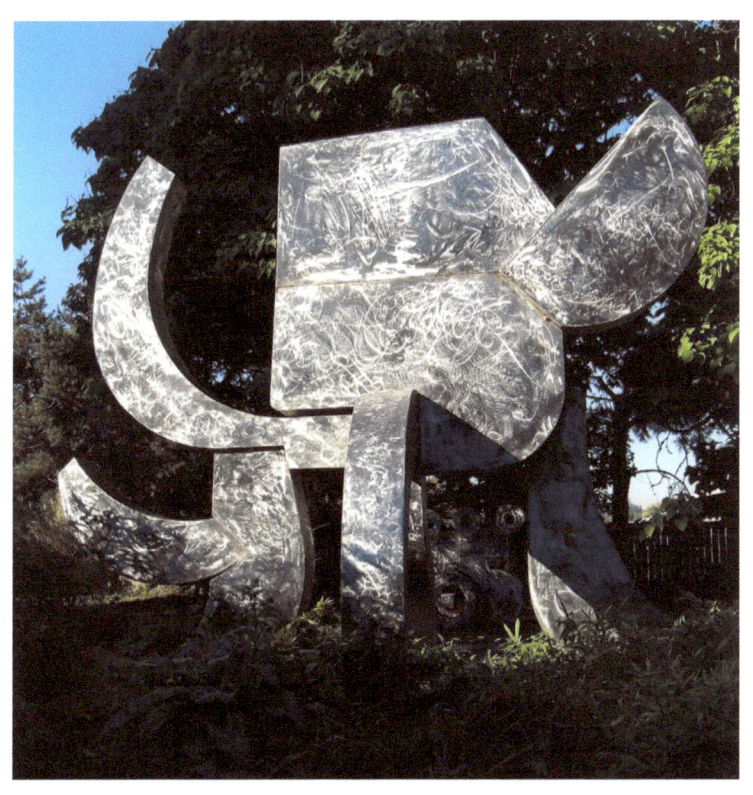

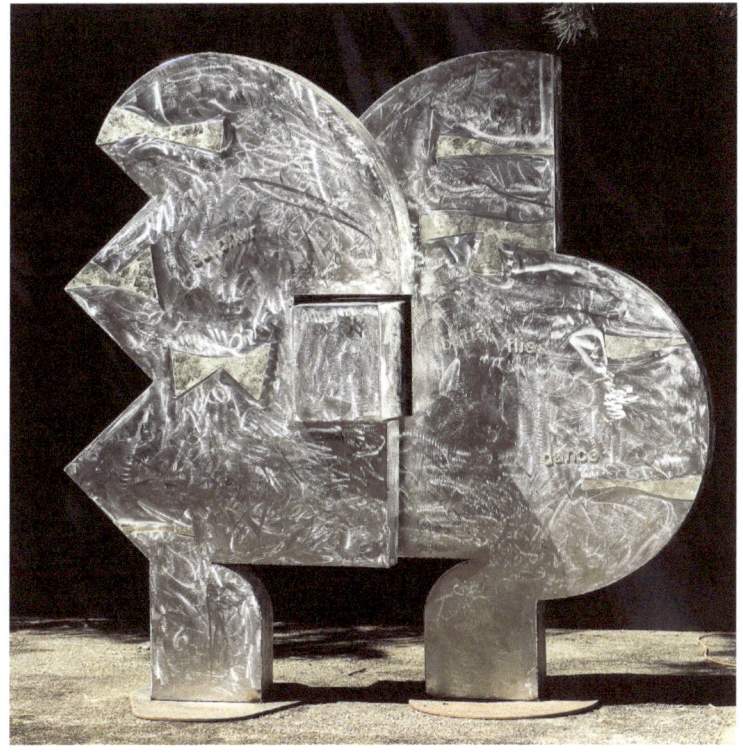

Kyoto 8 VIII 2007
Watercolor, collage and gold leaf on paper, 14.5 x 11 inches
Collection of the artist

Kyoto 8 I 2007
Watercolor, collage and gold leaf on paper, 14.5 x 11 inches
Private collection

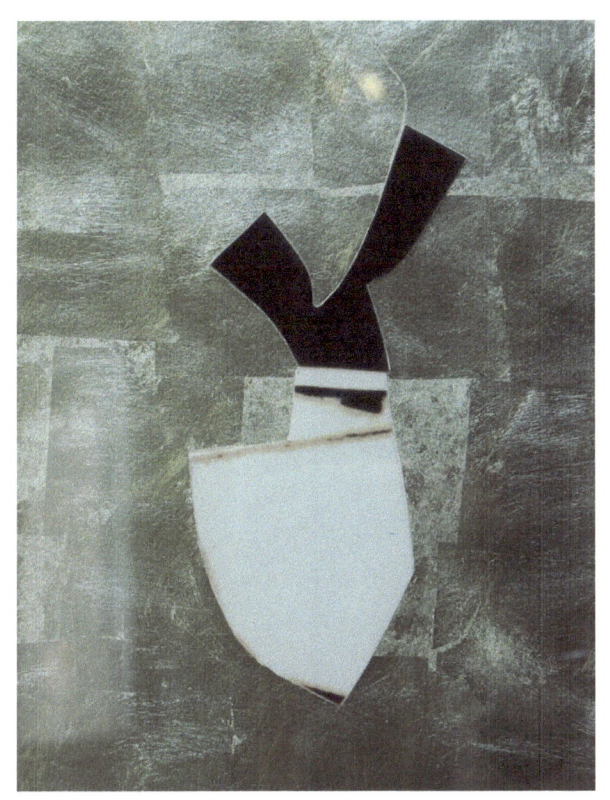

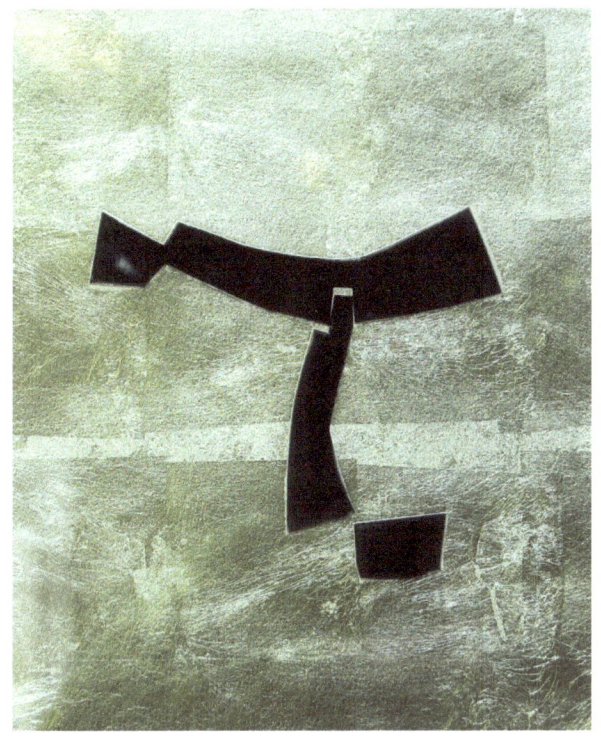

Kyoto (8) I 2--7
Painted steel, 40.5 x 20 x 6 inches
Collection of Mark and Ann Edlen

Kyoto 9 2007
Painted steel, 24 x 26 x 3 inches
Collection of GBD Architects

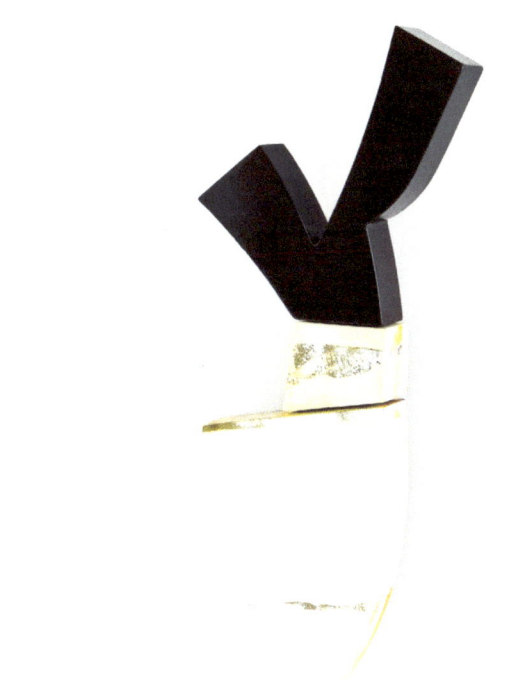

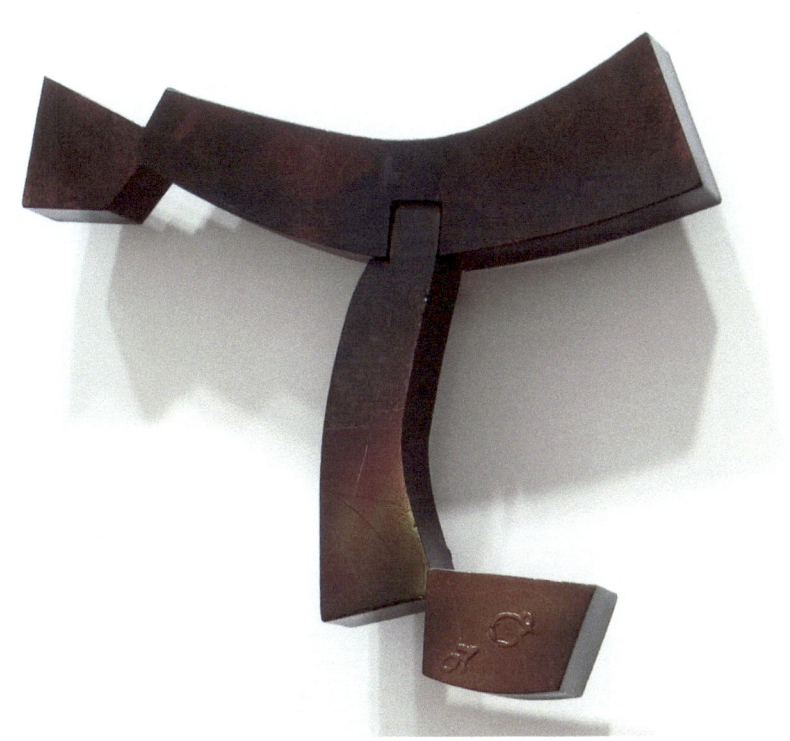

Doubtful Sound 4 2008
Welded steel with gold leaf, 35 x 27.25 x 3 inches
Collection of the artist

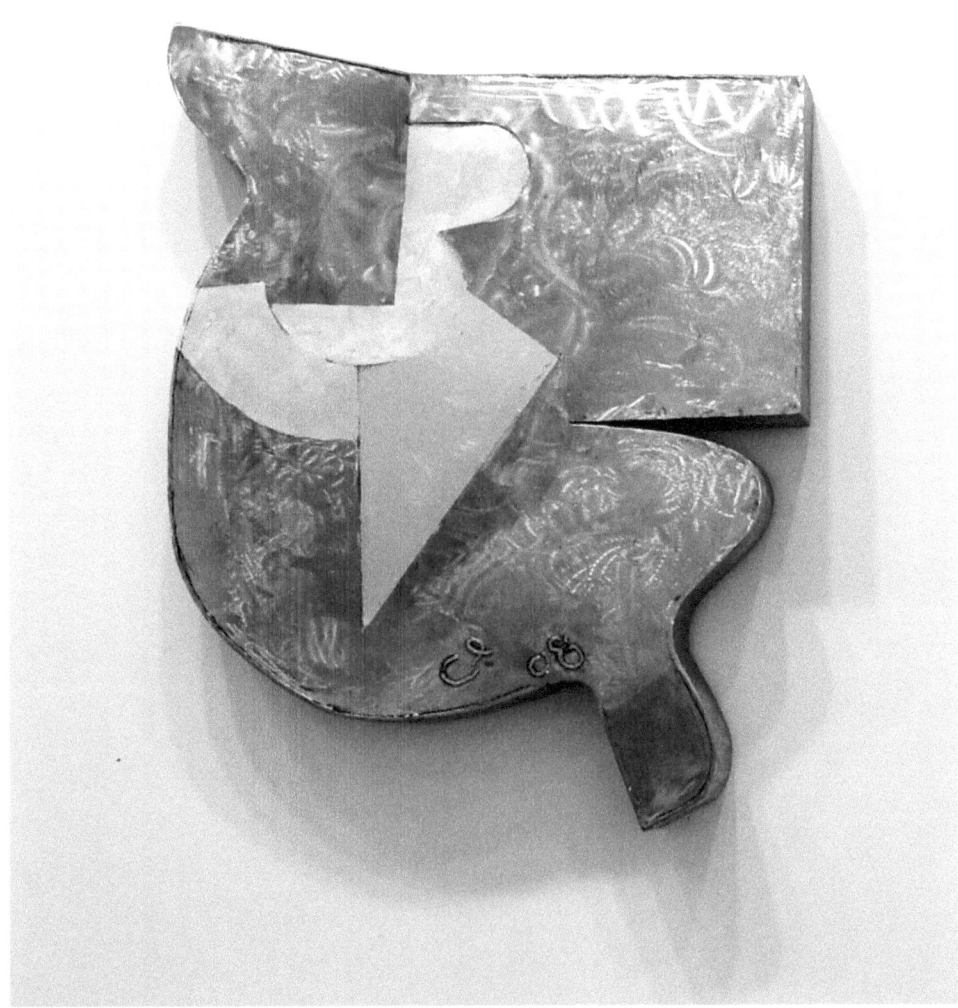

Bones Boxes "D" 2009
Stainless steel & wood with gold leaf, 24 x 24 x 4.75 inches
Collection of the artist

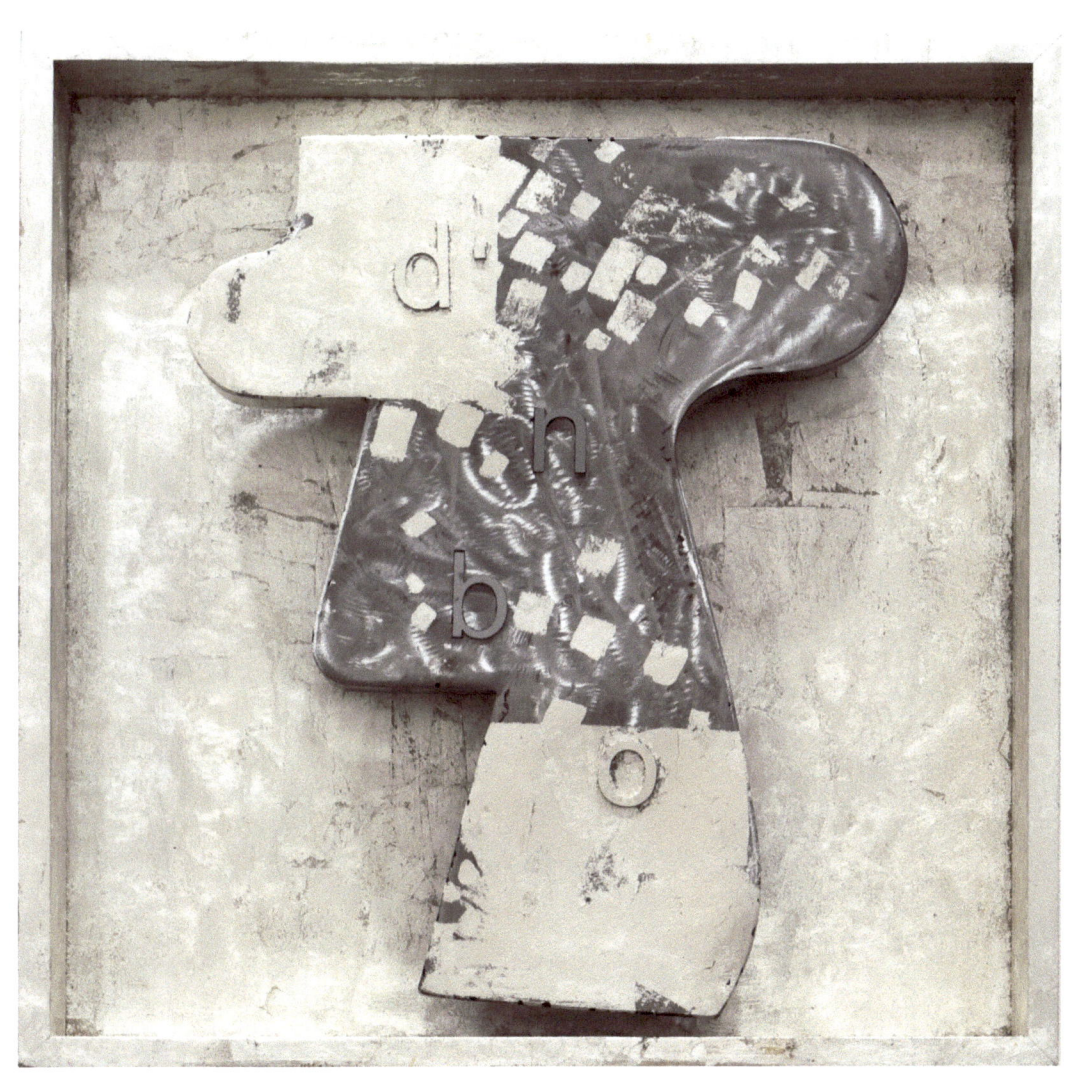

Clockwise, from top:

Goddess Glyphs I 2009
Steel & paint with gold leaf on panel, 9 x 9 x 1 inches
Private collection

Goddess Glyphs II 2009
Steel & paint with gold leaf on panel, 9 x 9 x 1 inches
Private collection

Goddess Glyphs V 2009
Steel & paint with gold leaf on panel, 9 x 9 x 1 inches
Collection of the artist

Goddess Glyphs VII 2009
Steel & paint with gold leaf on panel, 9 x 9 x 1 inches
Collection of the artist

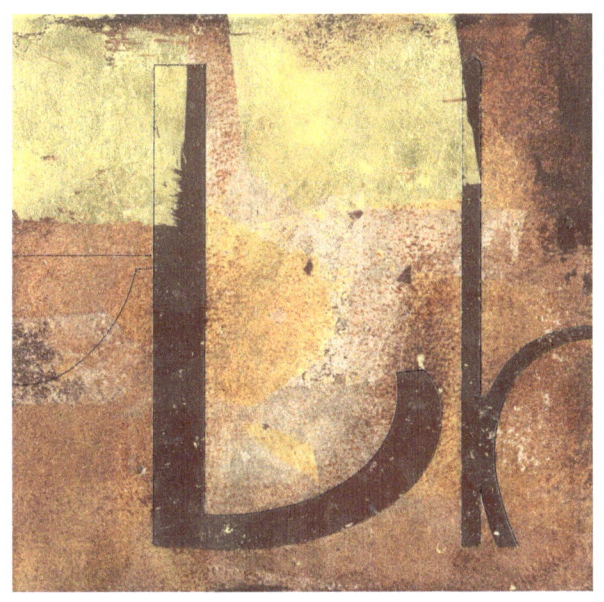 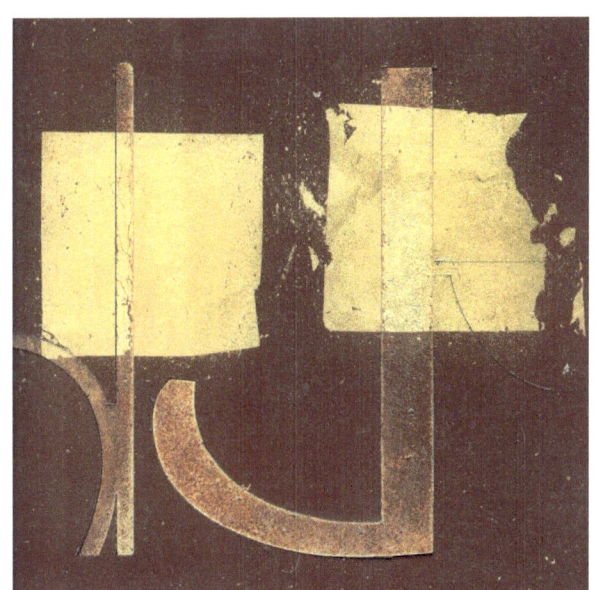

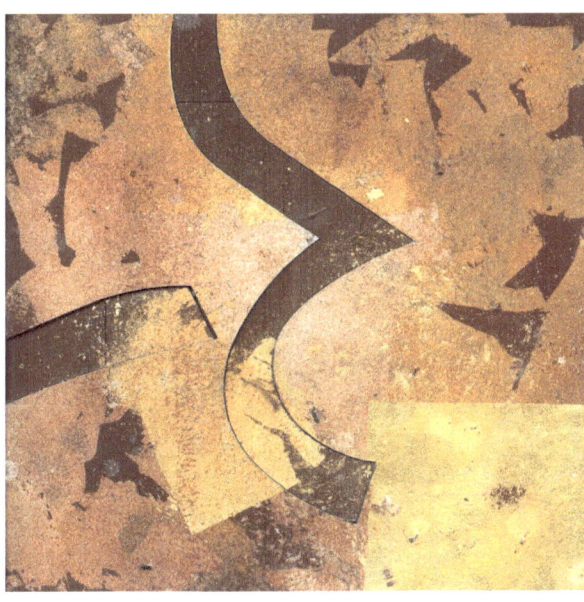 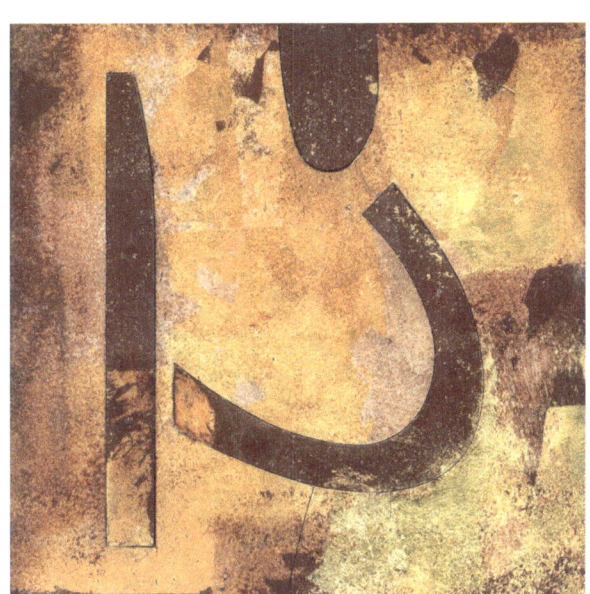

Goddess Revisited III 2009
Gold leaf and paint over welded steel
Collection of the artist

Goddess Revisited I 2009
Gold leaf and paint over welded steel
Collection of the artist

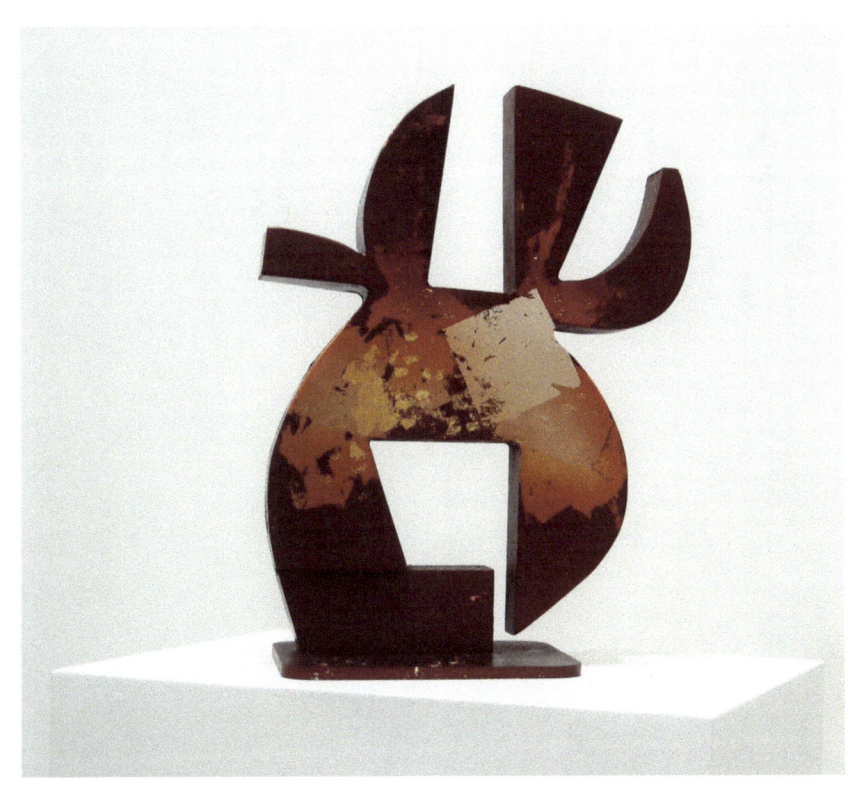

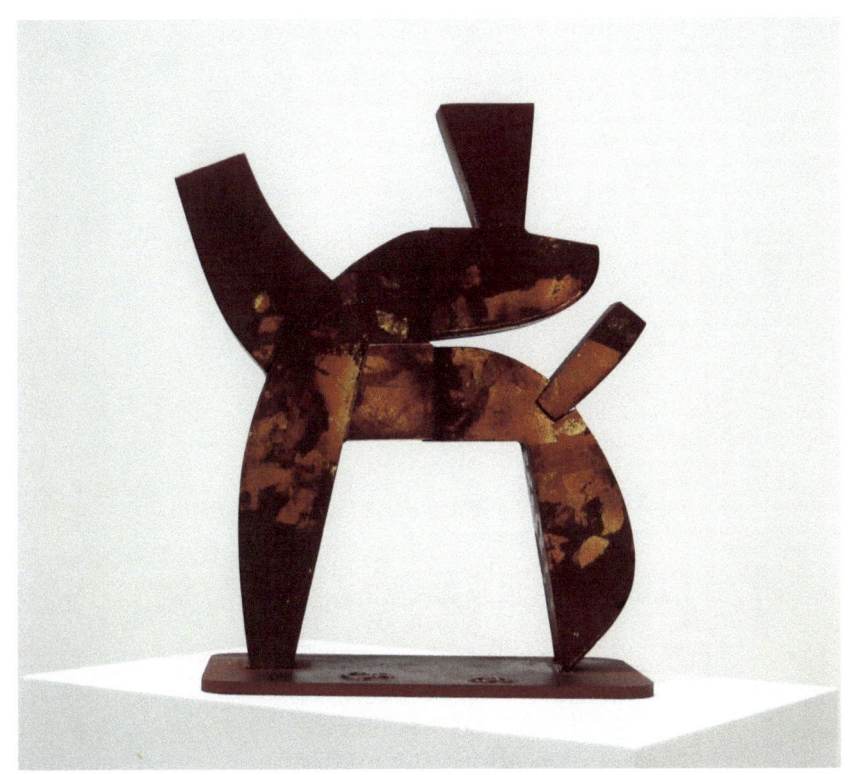

[Above]
Moontrap 2011
Stainless steel, 102 x 464 x 6 inches
Commissioned by the Rotary Club of Oregon City

[Below]
Two details of *Moontrap* 2011
Stainless steel, 102 x 464 x 6 inches
Commissioned by the Rotary Club of Oregon City

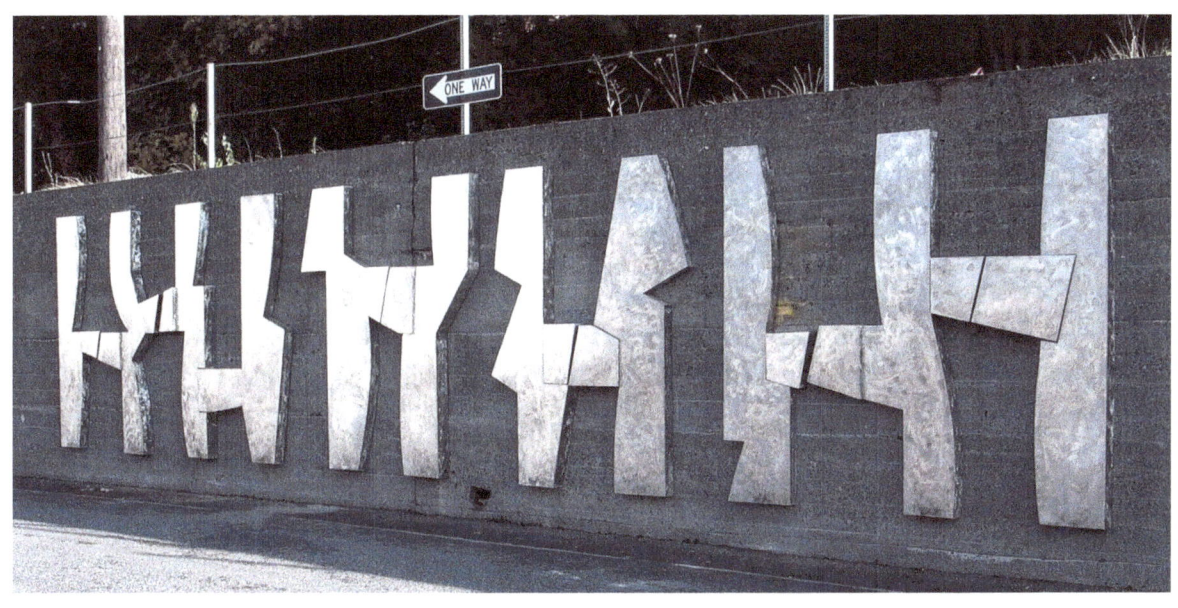

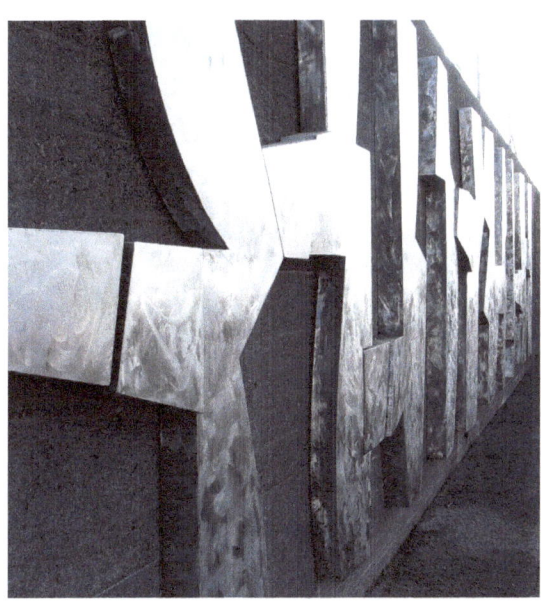
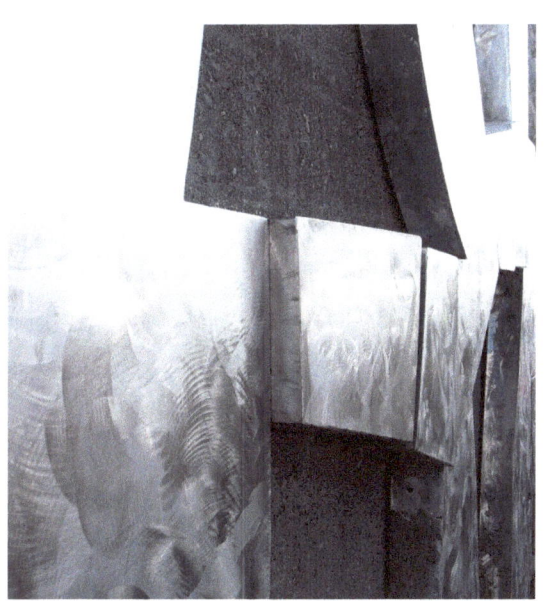

Pumalin I 2012
Weathered steel, 29 x 36 x 5.5 inches
Collection of Peter & Stephanie Sammons

Pumalin II 2012
Weathered steel, 34.5 x 23.5 x 5.5 inches
Collection of the artist

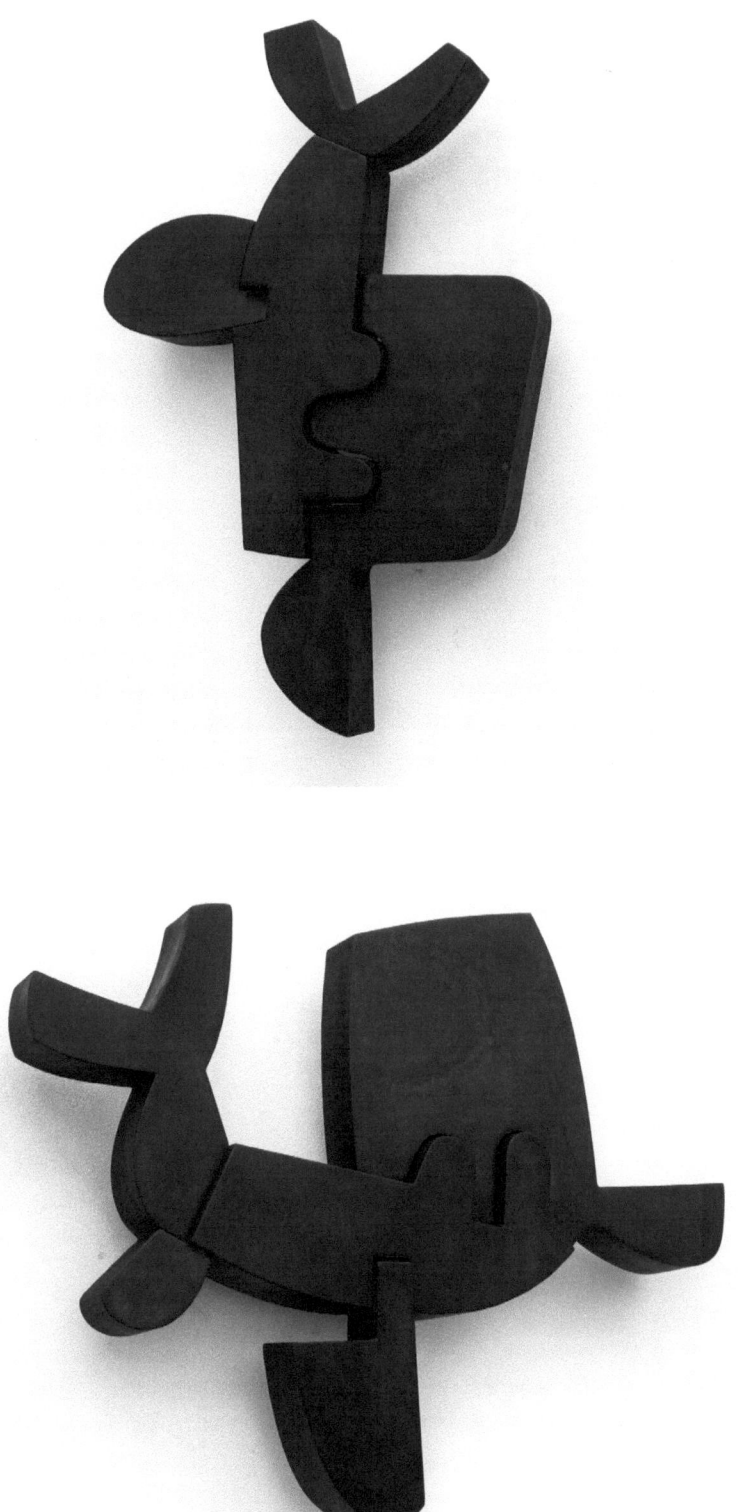

Atacama II 2012
Gold leaf over welded steel, 18 x 23.25 x 7 inches
Collection of Susan Hammer

Atacama IV 2012
Gold leaf over welded steel, 29 x 26.25 x 7 inches
Collection of Gard Communications

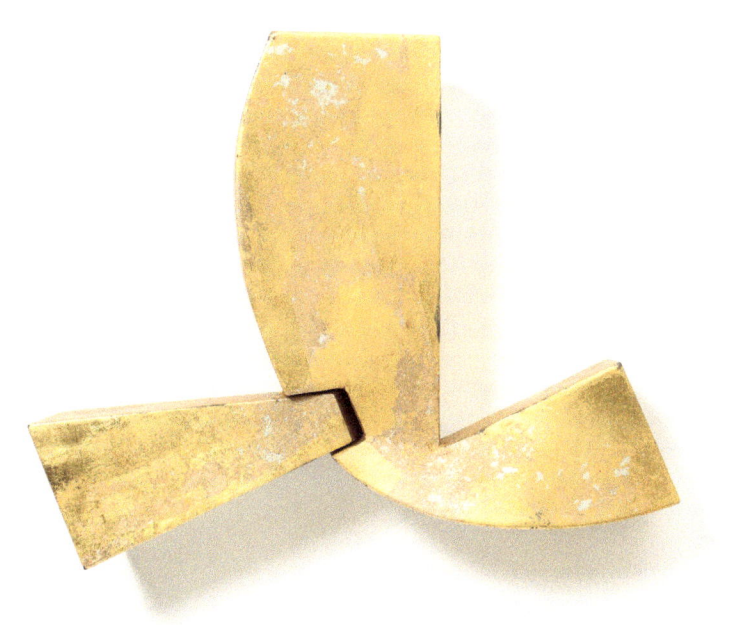
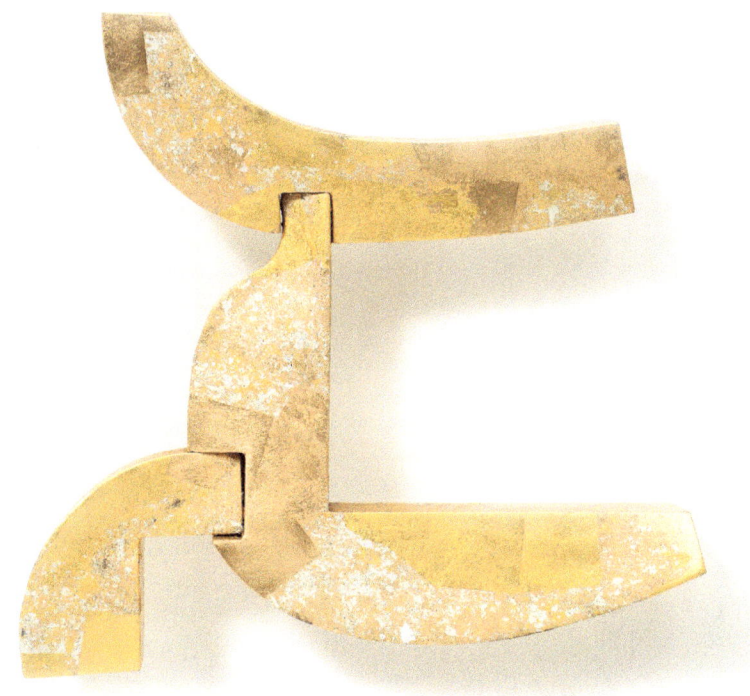

Pavilion II 2013
Stainless steel, 98 x 84 x 53 inches
Collection of the artist

Pavilion I 2013
Stainless steel, 64 x 50 x 34 inches
Collection of the artist

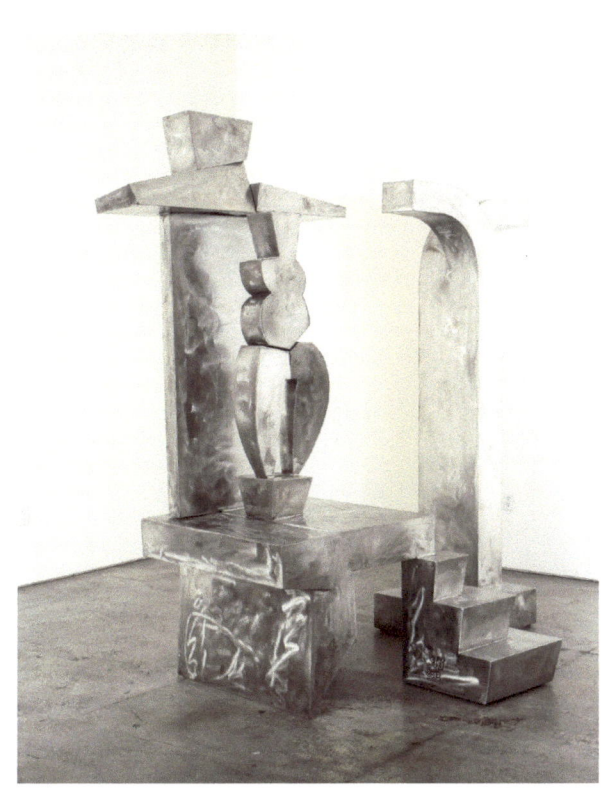

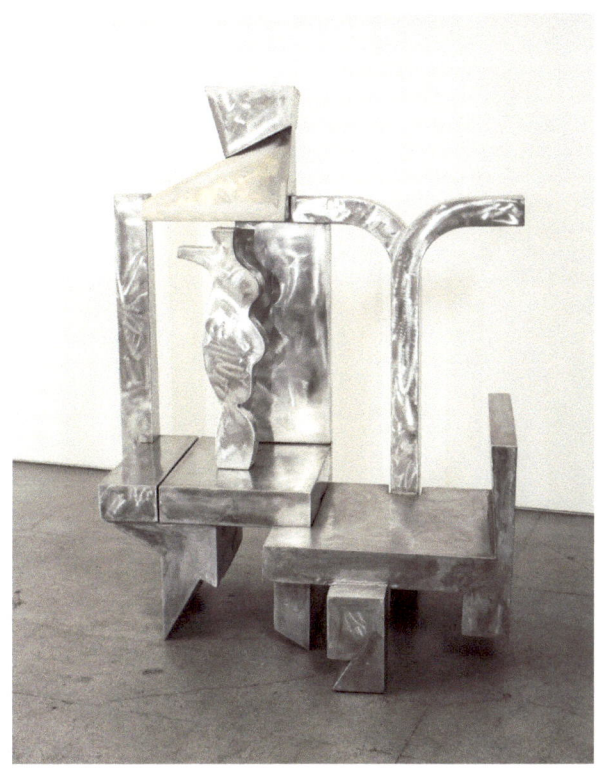

Lee Kelly   **Selected Solo Exhibitions, Commissions & Corporate Collections, 1990-2015**

2014   *Pavilion: New Painting and Sculpture*, Elizabeth Leach Gallery, Portland, Oregon.

2012   Commission for *Celebes*, wall sculpture, Vestas Corporation, Portland, Oregon.
         Purchase of *Memory 99*, Pacific Northwest College of Art & the Ford Family Foundation, Portland, Oregon.
         Atacama, Elizabeth Leach Gallery, Portland, Oregon.

2011   Commission for *Moontrap*, wall sculpture, Rotary Club, Oregon City, Oregon.
         Commission for *Rings*, Cor-ten steel sculpture, private residence, Portland, Oregon.
         Maquettes, Elizabeth Leach Gallery, Portland, Oregon.

2010   *Lee Kelly: A Retrospective*, Portland Art Museum, Portland, Oregon.
         Chrome Sculpture: 1967/2010, Elizabeth Leach Gallery, Portland, Oregon.
         Purchase of *Sound Garden*, Art in Public Places, Bend, Oregon.

2009   *Reflections of Khajuraho*, Elizabeth Leach Gallery, Portland, Oregon.
         Commission and purchase of *Bennington II* (2009) and *Blue Benn* (1998), Washington State Arts Commission
                  for Evergreen High School, Vancouver, Washington.
         Commission for *Untitled*, Solheim residence, Portland, Oregon.

2008   *Doubtful Sound*, Elizabeth Leach Gallery, Portland, Oregon.
         Commissioned stainless steel wall sculpture, West Portland Physical Therapy, Portland, Oregon.
         Purchase of *Ship of Renewal I*, Saks Fifth Avenue, New York, New York.

2007   Elizabeth Leach Gallery, Portland, Oregon.
         Civic Sculpture, B-Street Gallery, Portland, Oregon.
         Commission for *Howard's Way*, The Civic, Portland, Oregon.
         Commission for *Untitled*, Munch residence, Portland, Oregon.
         Purchase of *Kyoto 3, 7, 9 & 10*, Bellevue Towers, Bellevue, Washington.
         Purchase of *Kyoto 4*, The Casey Condominiums, Portland, Oregon.
         Purchase of *Sulawesi VII*, Quimby Corporation, Portland, Oregon.
         Commission for *Untitled*, Hockensmith & McCulloch residence, Portland, Oregon.
         Commission for *Untitled (Sulawesi Series)*, The John Ross Tower, Portland, Oregon.

2006   *Incidents of Travel: Sculptures and Works on Paper*, Elizabeth Leach Gallery, Portland, Oregon.
         Commission for *Tahoe*, Lemelson residence, Incline Village, Nevada.
         Commissioned stainless steel wall sculpture, Gustafson residence, Portland, Oregon.
         Commissioned wall sculpture, Johnson residence, Portland, Oregon.

2005   *Icarus Revisited: New Sculpture*, Elizabeth Leach Gallery, Portland, Oregon.
         Commission for *Loowit*, painted steel sculpture, Legacy Hospital, Vancouver Washington.
         Commission for *Fish Ladder*, sculptural fish ladder, Caldera, Blue Lake, Oregon,
                  in collaboration with the Oregon Department of Fish and Wildlife.
         Commission for *Sculpture in Two Parts*, Meridian Park Hospital, Tualatin, Oregon.
         Commission for *Nelson Irrigation*, Walla Walla, Washington.
         Commission for *Tri-Met #2*, Tri-Met, Beaverton, Oregon.
         Outdoor installation of *Angkor Weep*, Quimby Welding, Portland, Oregon.

2004	Commissioned indoor fountain, Portland Community College, Sylvania Campus.
	Commission for *Nancy's Garden*, private residence, Portland, Oregon.
	Purchase of *Angkor IV*, Whitman College, Walla Walla, Washington.
	Purchase of *Sulawesi VI*, M Financial, Portland, Oregon.
	Commission of *Untitled in Three Parts*, Davis & Johantgen residence, Portland, Oregon.
2003	Purchase of *Canakkale*, stainless steel, Carol Woodruff Plaza, Richland, Washington.
	Purchase of *Chalice I, II & III*, Gerding Edlen Development, Portland, Oregon.
2002	*Small Sculptures with Drawings*, Buckley Center Gallery, University of Portland, Portland, Oregon.
	Commissioned stainless steel wall sculpture for exterior of Box and One Lofts,
	Portland, Oregon (Kevin Cavanaugh, Fletcher, Farr, Ayotte, architects).
	Installation of two outdoor sculptures, *Lava Ridge* and *Four Columns*, Whitman College, Walla Walla, Washington.
2001	Commission for *Lupin Fugue*, stainless steel, Oregon Garden, Silverton, Oregon.
2000	*Travel Notes: Recent Sculpture*, Elizabeth Leach Gallery, Portland, Oregon.
	Commission for *Powell Fountain*, Powell residence, Portland, Oregon.
	Outdoor installation of *Lupin Study*, Hammer residence, Tacoma, Washington.
1999	*Trek to Sulawesi: Recent Wall Sculpture*, Fairbanks Gallery, Oregon State University, Corvallis, Oregon.
	Commission for *Healing Place*, St. Vincent Hospital, Portland, Oregon.
	Purchase of *Celebes Sea Snake Songs II*, FAIA, Portland, Oregon.
	Purchase of *Celebes*, CTC Consulting, Portland, Oregon.
1998	*Recent Wall Sculptures*, Oregon State University, Corvallis, Oregon.
	Ships of Renewal and Other New Work, Elizabeth Leach Gallery, Portland, Oregon.
	Commission for *Bend Gate*, City of Bend, Oregon.
	Commissioned sculpture, Sarkis residence, Seattle, Washington.
	Purchase of *Naga*, Oregon State University, Corvallis, Oregon.
	Purchase of *Sulawesi I*, Oregon State University, Corvallis, Oregon.
1997	Elizabeth Leach Gallery, Portland, Oregon.
1996	*New Print Editions*, 21 Steps Print Studio, Portland, Oregon.
	Purchase of *Seljuk*, Cor-ten steel, Reed College, Portland, Oregon. Gift of Don Frisbee.
	Purchase of *Angkor Series #1-94*, bronze over steel, Goodman residence, Portland, Oregon.
	Purchase of *Untitled*, Stanford University Hospital, Palo Alto, California.
1995	Commission for *Stainless Dreaming*, Portland Community College, Rock Creek campus, Portland, Oregon.
	Commission for *Salmon River*, Portland-Sapporo Sister City Program. Sapporo, Japan.
1994	*Lee Kelly: 35 Years of Painting and Sculpture*, The Art Gym, Marylhurst College, Marylhurst, Oregon.
	Purchase of *Summer Songs 1 & 2*, Fletcher, Farr & Ayotte, Portland, Oregon.
1993	*Collaborations in Steel and Sound*, Cheney Cowles Museum, Spokane, Washington.
	With composer Michael Stirling.
	Sound Garden, Elizabeth Leach Gallery, Portland, Oregon.
1992	*Tools of the Butter Trade*, Elizabeth Leach Gallery, Portland, Oregon.
	Purchase of *Stainless Garden*, Stanford University, Palo Alto, California.

Lee Kelly is represented by Elizabeth Leach Gallery, Portland, Oregon. More at www.elizabethleach.com.

Lee Kelly   **Selected Biography**

2010   *Lee Kelly: A Retrospective*, Portland Art Museum, Portland, Oregon.
2008   Travel to New Zealand.
2006   Travel to Japan: Kyoto, Naoshima, Tokyo.
2006   Travel to Haida sites, Queen Charlotte Islands.
2005   Travel to Patagonia, Argentina & Chile.
2004   Travel to India & Sri Lanka.
2003   Travel to Anasazi sites, American Southwest.
2000   Travel to Burma and Nepal.
1994   Travels in Cambodia and Thailand. Visiting artist to Sapporo, Japan, as part of Portland-
           Sapporo Sister City Program.
           Lee Kelly: Thirty-five years of Painting and Sculpture, The Art Gym, Marylhurst College,
           Marylhurst, Oregon.
1992   Masters Fellowship in Sculpture, State of Oregon.
1987   Oregon Governor's Award for the Arts.
1985   Oregon Arts Commission Fellowship to research traditional bronze casting methods
           of the Newari of Nepal.
1984   *Lee Kelly: Outdoor Sculpture*, The Art Gym, Marylhurst College, Marylhurst, Oregon.
1979   First visit to Nepal and India.
1976-79 Visiting Professor of Art, Reed College, Portland, Oregon.

Photo Credits

Frontispiece: courtesy Elizabeth Leach Gallery and Dan Kvitka
page 2: courtesy Elizabeth Leach Gallery and Dan Kvitka
pages 7 through 23: courtesy Elizabeth Leach Gallery and Dan Kvitka
page 33: courtesy Lee Kelly Stodio
pages 35 through 37: courtesy Elizabeth Leach Gallery and Dan Kvitka
page 39: courtesy Elizabeth Leach Gallery
page 41: courtesy Elizabeth Leach Gallery and Dan Kvitka
page 43: courtesy Lee Kelly Stoio and Randal Davis
page 4S: courtesy Elizabeth Leach Gallery and Dan Kvitka
page 47: courtesy Lee Kelly Studio and Randal Davis
pages 49 through 53: courtesy Elizabeth Leach Gallery and Dan Kvitka
page 61: courtesy Elizabeth Leach Gallery and Dan Kvitka

Clockwise from top left:
Study for a Painting I 2014
Collage on gesso board, 11 x 9 inches
Collection of the artist

Study for a Painting II 2014
Collage on gesso board, 11 x 9 inches
Collection of the artist

Study for a Painting III 2014
Collage on gesso board, 11 x 9 inches
Collection of the artist

Study for a Painting IV 2014
Collage on gesso board, 11 x 9 inches
Private collection

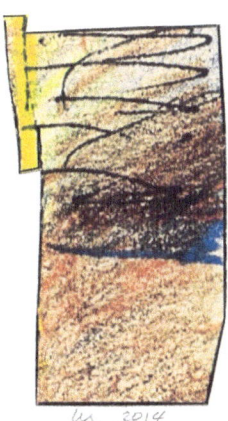

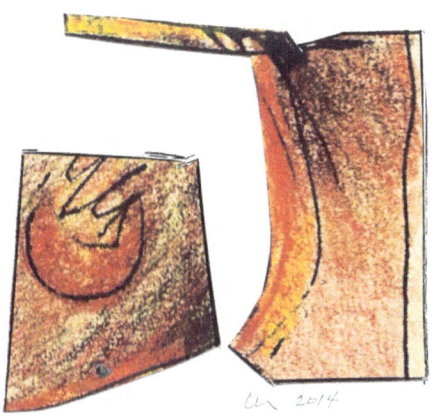

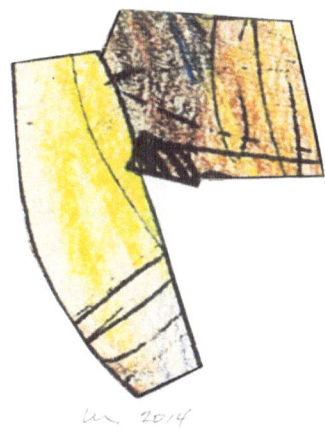

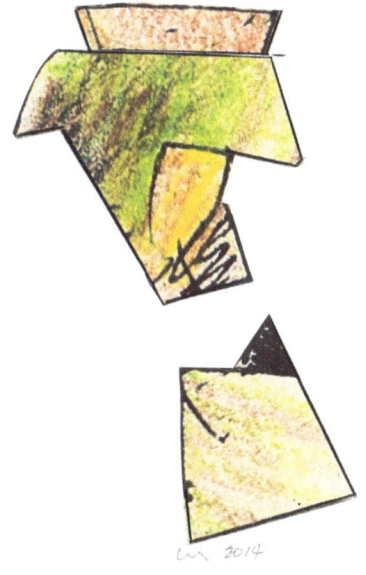

www.ingramcontent.com/pod-product-compliance
Lightning Source LLC
Chambersburg PA
CBHW050751180526
45159CB00003B/1427

* 9 781517 513429 *